The Secret of Love

A Glimpse into the Mystical Wisdom of Rav Kook

Aryeh Ben David

Kasva Press

St. Paul / Alfei Menashe

Book design & layout: Yael Shahar

Author photo: Debbi Cooper

First edition published 2023
Kasva Press LLC
www.kasvapress.com
Alfei Menashe, Israel / St. Paul, Minnesota
info@kasvapress.com

The Secret of Love
ISBN
Trade Paperback: 978-1-948403-41-2
Ebook: 978-1-948403-42-9

9 8 7 6 5 4 3 2 1

For my family – Sandra, kids & spouses, and grandkids –
you keep inviting me to love more.

For my Ayeka Community –
How wonderful, blessed, and sacred to journey together.

Contents

The Secret of Love

Introduction

This is a book about love. To be more exact, it is a book about how to become a more loving human being — about how to love ourselves, our families, our communities, other human beings, and all of creation — more. It has been inspired by the writings of the contemporary mystic, Rabbi Avraham Yitzchak HaCohen Kook, usually referred to as Rav Kook.

I am in my sixties, and until recently, I never knew that I could grow in my loving. My wife, Sandra, is an extremely loving person. It comes naturally to her. She wakes up in the morning already thinking about what she can do for our children, our grandchildren, and others.

I'm not like that. I live in my head. I live in the world of ideas. And while I have said countless times to my wife, "I love you," I would not consider myself an especially loving person. People would probably say that I am a nice guy, perhaps friendly and considerate, but "loving" is not a word that would pop into their heads when they think of me.

I have studied the ideas of Rav Kook for the last 40 years, but in the fall of 2020, as part of an online community, I began to delve more deeply into his writings. A deep dive. I allowed all the holy books on my shelves to gather dust as I focused exclusively on Rav Kook's approach to living a Jewish life. It was Rav Kook, all day, every day. During this time, something in me changed; something shifted. I became more loving.

I feel it. My kids notice it. Others have told me. My heart has become more expansive. I have more patience and compassion. I judge people more positively. I listen better. The small steps that I have taken so far have been very rewarding, deepening my sense of gratitude and well-being. I feel healthier, both physically and spiritually.

I observe this process with a bit of shock. What happened?

These changes took place without a plan. They were not intentional. And yet, they didn't just happen. Rav Kook happened.

To be clear, I don't have any illusions of being a paragon of love. I don't expect to win the Nobel Prize for loving. I still don't come up to the ankles of my wife. My aspirations are very small. I just want to continue to take small steps in expanding and deepening my love for all human beings and all of creation. During the last few years while discussing this with others, it has become apparent to me that I am not alone in this desire.

> "Who is the most loving person you know?" What wouldn't all of us give to be the answer to that question?

At our Friday night Shabbat dinner, we once asked: "Who is the most loving person you know?" All eight of us — our six kids, my wife and myself — immediately responded with the same person: "Sabi", my wife's father. And it got me thinking — what wouldn't all of us give to be the answer to that question? Wouldn't all of us find it incredibly rewarding if people referred to us as the most loving person they knew? Wouldn't that include just about all the praiseworthy traits and behaviors that we try so hard to embody?

And even more than becoming more loving human beings in our personal relationships — don't we sense that the larger world today is in desperate need of more love? The brokenness and anger present in Jewish life seems irreparable. Jews from different religious denominations and ideological views cannot sit together, much less respect each other's positions and love each other. Our political arena has become toxic and awash with animosity.

And that is why I wanted to write this book: to share with others Rav Kook's approach to the centrality of love in Jewish life.

Though this may not be what we learned in school or synagogue, I'm writing this book for us to understand that becoming a more loving human being is really what Judaism is all about.

There was a specific moment recently when I realized that I needed to write this book — a moment of love that transpired solely because of the effect that Rav Kook's wisdom had on my life.

Over thirty years ago, when I was starting out on my professional career, I received my first teaching position. Sandra and I had two little kids at the time, and we lived in a small apartment in Jerusalem. I was grateful for the job, even though I was starting at the bottom of the teaching ladder. The director generously took a chance on me and gave me a few hours for minimal pay. Everyone else on the staff knew much more than I did and had many more years of teaching experience. They seemed like giants to me. After several years, I received more hours and a larger teaching portfolio. I started to become grounded in my teaching approach and my relationship with the students.

My fourth year was especially successful. I poured myself into the job, putting in countless extra hours. I went on all the hikes, showed up at the extracurricular activities, and invited almost all of the students for Shabbat meals. A major investment in every way.

At the end of the year, we were notified of our teaching hours for the upcoming year. I was shocked to learn that my hours had been slashed. "The director is worried about your becoming too popular," one of the senior teachers privately disclosed to me.

> Though this may not be what we learned in school or synagogue, becoming a more loving human being is really what Judaism is all about.

I was distraught. Sandra and I wouldn't have enough money to pay our rent and I had no idea where I could find other teaching opportunities. Complete panic set in. I wondered if I had brought this on myself by being too critical of some of the educational policies during the weekly staff meetings.

I asked to talk with the director. He invited me into his large office where he sat behind a magnificent antique desk that felt like a moat between the two of us. He was many years ahead of me in life. He had power; I had none. Reaching for the handle of the door to enter his office, I noticed that my body was uncontrollably shaking. Throughout the entire meeting, I could not stop trembling.

He began to lecture me, explaining how he runs the institution, why he does what he does. He said he cut my hours because he had to consider what was best for the whole staff and the school. He claimed that it was not personal. From his tone I wasn't so sure. He wished me well. I left feeling empty, of meager worth. My whole future in Jewish education had been shredded.

Many years passed. We occasionally saw each other at conferences but only nodded or gave a non-commital shrug.

Recently we saw that his wife, after a long illness, had passed away. We had not been in contact for over twenty-five years. For me, the scars of our encounters had never healed; the pain and anger were still easily triggered.

I said to Sandra that we should pay a shiva call. It would entail a journey of several hours, but for some reason it was clear to me that we should make the trip. When we walked into his home, visible surprise crossed his face. I was probably one of the last people he expected to see.

Sandra and I sat down next to him. After moments of consoling him about his wife, I interrupted the conversation to say to him,

> I'm writing this book to share Rav Kook's insights and help others channel the deep mystical wisdom of a master of love.

4

"There's something I want to tell you. We were once close and I know we had bumps in our relationship. I was young and probably caused a few of them. I want to tell you now that I am sorry and to ask forgiveness for whatever role I played in messing things up."

Sandra's jaw dropped in disbelief. She knew all too well how traumatic that time had been, and what I had carried for so many years. He paused for a moment in disbelief, and then responded, "Well, I'm sure I also played a role in those bumps. I'm sorry too. I'm glad you made it here. We should get together."

We talked for a few more minutes and then bid our farewells.

After years of harboring resentment and anger, I was able to just let it go. It was not an effort. Somewhere, deep inside, I knew that I had to invite peace into our relationship and be a force of healing, oneness, and love. I genuinely look forward to spending time with him again.

On the ride home, I realized that I would never have felt or acted like this if I had not been studying the writings of Rav Kook. I noticed with some surprise and pleasure that his wisdom had apparently begun to penetrate into my heart and soul.

It was then that I realized I needed to write about Rav Kook. I wanted to share his insights and help others channel the deep mystical wisdom of a master of love.

> I would never have felt or acted as a more loving person if I had not been studying the writings of Rav Kook.

How to Read this Book

This is a book where the most important moments for the reader occur before and after its reading.

Before Learning

In this book, the most important moments occur before and after the reading.

Shemoneh Kvatzim 6:107

Rav Kook writes:

> *The success of learning*
> *is dependent on its connection*
> *to the natural living inner spark*
> *of one's soul.*

What is "success" in learning?

For years, I made the terrible mistake of believing that the goal of learning was to know more and more content. I dove into studying without preparation or forethought. Other than quickly knocking off the traditional blessing recited before opening the holy books, there was no deliberate transition to learning. There was no inner formative process. While studying, I frantically raced to cover as much material as I could. I learned without awareness or consideration of the role that the learning could possibly play in my life. It was an intellectual experience; I falsely assumed that the acquisition of knowledge was sufficient to benefit my soul. Success was measured by how many pages of Talmud I mastered.

When I look back, I realize that my learning was completely disengaged from relationships. My study partner in yeshiva, Lior, had three small children. One of their kids had health issues and Lior almost never got a full night's sleep. Once, after learning with Lior all morning, I came home for lunch and Sandra asked me how Lior

6

and his wife were coping with the situation. I looked at her in disbelief. "I have no idea how they're doing," I said. "We're learning. We're not going to take time for personal stuff". Learning was completely disconnected from life.

Rav Kook had a very different take on learning. It wasn't just about the amount of knowledge absorbed. Learning was more than an intellectual endeavor. For Rav Kook, learning was a soulful experience, a means to the goal of growing spiritually and clarifying one's path in life. Special spiritual preparation was a prerequisite in order to avoid turning the experience into an exclusively intellectual process.

Rav Kook writes:

> *According to the quality and clarity of one's yearning*
> *to grow soulfully and improve before learning —*
> *will be the depth and clarity of the learning.*

Yearning to be affected by our learning not only ensures that the content will be integrated into our lives, it also deepens the quality of the learning itself. Before he began to learn, Rav Kook would direct his "natural living inner spark" to be open and receptive to personalizing what he was about to learn. Just as prayer requires proper focus and *kavanah* (direction), so too, learning requires soulful preparation.

In order to help us align our learning with Rav Kook's approach, I have offered a trigger question ("Yearning to Grow") at the beginning of each chapter. This question is aimed at opening ourselves up to personal growth and to connecting the learning to our "living inner spark".

Yearning to be affected by our learning not only ensures that the content will be integrated into our lives, it also deepens the quality of the learning itself.

Orot HaTorah 6:2

Questions we should ask ourselves as we begin reading this book are:

* *How ready am I to reflect on my life?*

* *What is holding me back from growing soulfully?*

* *What advice would I give to myself to become more receptive to new ideas?*

* *How much do I want to become a more loving person?*

After Learning

The most important moment in any learning occurs after the learning is over. Learning is the preparation for the personalization, integration, and implementation of new ideas.

After learning, Rav Kook advised himself:

> *I am demanded by my soul,*
> *after every period of study…*
> *to liberate myself*
> *from the spiritual chains*
> *which imprison my soul,*
> *and to wander freely*
> *in all of the worlds,*
> *guided by the concealed spark of the subjects*
> *I have just learned.*

Rav Kook is inviting us to pause and reflect after "every period of study". This process is not just a praiseworthy option, it is "demanded" by our souls.

Rav Kook uses this expression "demanded by my soul" often. "Demanded" is very strong language. It denotes an unstoppable inner

---
Rav Kook is inviting us to pause and reflect after every period of study.

SHK 8:171]

drive within us, relentless and forceful. The soul is beseeching us to pay attention. The soul is demanding that we listen to it.

When Rav Kook talks about being *demanded by his soul* to free himself of his spiritual chains, he is giving voice to the yearning of his soul. The soul cannot remain static; the soul abhors the status quo. It is pleading with him to continue to wrestle, to evolve, to grow, and to journey — to fulfill its destiny in this world. Paradoxically, all previous breakthroughs in learning — all previous steps of growth brought about through study — can subsequently imprison us in "spiritual chains", holding us back from continuing to change and grow. Yesterday's success can become today's impediment.

In the world of education, I have witnessed this phenomenon of "spiritual chains" countless times. One of my colleagues would teach the exact same course, replete with the same stories and jokes, for decades. Students loved his course, but Rav Kook might say that he had become stuck, imprisoned by his own success. Personally, I have found it so safe and comfortable to rely on previous scripts and ideas which resonated with the students. It is all too easy to become entrapped and just repeat the past.

Rav Kook struggles never to become complacent in his learning, never to become too satisfied with his personal steps of development. He demands of himself that he grow. He needs to "wander freely in all of the worlds".

When Rav Kook ruminates on "wander(ing) freely in all of the worlds", he is summoning himself to explore new ideas without any prior strategy or design. To be completely free and open. He needs to "wander" — vulnerably and without constraint — to wherever and however these ideas may choose to manifest themselves in his life. He has no charted course nor blueprint; he wanders "freely", giving full and open expression to all possibilities.

> All previous breakthroughs in learning can subsequently imprison us in "spiritual chains", holding us back from continuing to change and grow. Yesterday's success can become today's impediment.

I strongly suggest that after reading each chapter of this book you take a moment to enter into this "wandering" space of Rav Kook. Ask yourselves the following questions:

* What piece of this learning personally resonated for me?

* How can this learning unsettle my status quo?

* How can this learning impact my life and help me to change?

* What small step can I take to leave my comfort zone?

To help liberate ourselves from the chains which imprison our souls, I have added two sections at the end of each chapter.

At the end of each chapter is a section ("Wandering freely") giving us an extra opportunity to reflect on the writings of Rav Kook and see what they evoke in us. This moment of reflection invites us to reflect and "wander freely in all of the worlds, guided by the concealed spark of the objects we have just learned".

Additionally, I have added personal questions and tasks ("Connecting to our Lives") inviting us to bring the learning into our lives and connect it to all we are doing. Again, the most important moment in learning occurs after the learning is over.

How can this learning impact my life and help me to change?

My Love Affair
with Rav Kook

I don't know where to begin other than to say that this book is a love story. Years ago I fell in love with Rav Kook. I am still in love with him.

I have a picture of Rav Kook hanging in my study. Rav Kook wore a black coat and fur hat (shtreimel). Once, a student entered my study, noticed the picture, and asked if it was my grandfather. I could not stop laughing. My grandfather, bless his soul, would go to Yom Kippur services with a small transistor radio in his pocket and an earphone running through his sleeve so he could listen to the World Series game during the rabbi's sermon! I don't think that he and Rav Kook had much in common. But then I paused and thought about it a bit more. "Yes," I answered. "Perhaps I can consider Rav Kook to be my spiritual grandparent."

Rav Kook (1865-1935) passed away twenty years before I was born, so of course I never met him. I know him only through his writings and the stories told about him. In 1904, he made aliyah to Israel, living in Old Jaffa. After World War I, he moved to Jerusalem where he lived for the rest of his life.

If you go to Rav Kook's house in Jerusalem, you can still see his study, with his large wooden desk. And if you look closely at the surface of the desk, you may discover the indentations of his writing.

Rav Kook wrote and wrote and wrote. Legend has it that he would line up sharpened pencils on the edge of his desk. He chose not to use a quill feather, the common practice of his time, as he didn't want to take the time to pause and dip the quill into the ink. "The thoughts come faster than the pen," he wrote. "Thoughts come faster than the hand can write." He couldn't stop writing. Sometimes there was not enough paper, and he would continue writing directly onto his desk.

Rav Kook was a giant in all branches of Jewish learning. When he was 17 years old, he lamented to his father that he didn't feel he was progressing, despite having finished the whole Talmud eight times that year! He was a scholar. He was a rabbi. He was a public figure. He wrote articles and commentaries; he even started a newspaper. He engaged with the most controversial political and religious issues of his time. He drew up plans for a trail-blazing yeshiva syllabus. He wrote volumes of letters, giving advice to people from all over the world. Yet his most personal and revealing writing is to be found outside of his more scholarly works

Over the course of more than 15 years, Rav Kook composed his private diaries, the *Shemoneh Kvatzim* (Eight Diaries, referred to here as SHK). These writings stemmed not from his mind, nor even from his heart, but from the depths of his soul, often shrouded in a mystical trance, and composed after midnight in the privacy of his study. He wrote from his soul to himself. Only decades after Rav Kook's passing were the *Shemoneh Kvatzim* released to the public.

We now have the priceless opportunity to glimpse into the inner life of a Jewish mystic. His writing in the *Shemoneh Kvatzim* was completely unfiltered. It was raw and vulnerable, complex and unsystematic. The *Shemoneh Kvatzim* are the diaries of Rav Kook's inner

> Rav Kook was a giant in all branches of Jewish learning. Yet his most personal and revealing writing is to be found outside of his more scholarly works.

life — the wanderings, aspirations, ecstasy and anguish of his soul.

The first thing we need to know about Rav Kook is that, at the root of his soul, he was a poet.

Perhaps this is what kindled my love for his writings. I have dabbled in poetry for most of my life. A high school teacher once asked us to write a poem, and I sat by the duck pond near our home for hours in solitude and reflection. That experience changed my life. Even today, I have weekly poetry sessions with our children and grandchildren. I needed a religious figure with a poetic soul, someone who evoked my inner stirrings. Rav Kook supplied that need.

What is a poet?

According to Rav Kook, a poet is one who listens to the mysterious inner melodies of the universe. The universe is alive. It is dynamic. It has a soul. There is a mystical melody resonating through it. The universe is singing in a spiritual harmony that is always calling to us from the heavens. We refer to God as "the living God," and the universe is breathing, flowing, evolving, and fully vibrant.

What does a poetic soul do? A poet listens to this music — to the soulful inner melody of the universe. A poet is attentive to the divine conversation happening every moment, pulsating throughout creation. The soul of a poet is inspired by the vibrations of the universe. The soul of a poet is in motion!

The poet does not intentionally construct poetry; there is no clear goal to his writing. Poetry simply emerges from the soul of the poet. Rav Kook did not plan most of his writing. He did not have an intentional or orderly style. He wrote the thoughts that were mystically conveyed to him by the soul of the universe. His words were evoked by the harmonic vibrations coming from the melody and harmony of God's universe. His poetry was a response to the musical invitation of the heavens.

> According to Rav Kook, a poet is one who listens to the mysterious inner melodies of the universe.

Those who listen for the discreet musings
beyond the worlds,
For each echoing note and chord,
Grasp the resonances in the light of dusk,
As the vestiges of light dim and pass.

And so he wrote. And wrote. And wrote. In the *Shemoneh Kvatzim*, there are thousands of entries — entries so deep and profound that countless scholars have spent their lives trying to decipher his thoughts.

Rav Kook's manuscripts reveal an astonishing truth: he virtually never edited his writing! We can see from the original pages of his diaries how he rarely rewrote a sentence, or even a word. He wrote as the waves and rushes of inspiration came to him, often creating new Hebrew words to express what he needed to say. He wrote that angels were continually knocking on his door.

And what did he write about?

Rav Kook wrote as the waves and rushes of inspiration came to him.

He wrote extensively about God, about the Jewish People, and about the land of Israel. He wrote about how we should learn Torah in a new way. He wrote about prayer and holiness. He wrote about how we can refine our qualities and expand our kindness. He wrote about aesthetics, exercise, and nature. He wrote about other religions, evolution, and scientific methodology and discoveries. He wrote about the nature of the soul and the soul of the universe. And he wrote at length about his relationship with the Creator of the world.

He wrote about the inner composition of his will. He wrote about his purpose and destiny in life. He wrote of his own moods — of his ecstasy, distress, and sorrow.

Alas, who can describe my pain?
Who will be a violin to express the songs of my grief?
Who will voice my bitterness,
my pain of seeking to fully express myself? . . .

How can I utter the great truth that fills my heart,
the sparkles filled with treasures of light and warmth,
which are stored inside my soul?

SHK 3:280

In the annals of Jewish writing — centuries of scholastic essays and untold books — Rav Kook's Eight Diaries are a unique undertaking. They offer a glimpse into the most raw and personal reflections of a mystic scholar who wrote about love, fear, and desire from the depths of the soul, with no consideration of how this writing would be received.

Certainly, it would have been much easier to understand Rav Kook if he had written in a systematic or linear style. It is heart-breaking that much of his writings are so obscure and impenetrable that the beauty, depth, and originality of his thought is lost for most of the Jewish world.

Yet, there was a reason that Rav Kook wrote the way he did. The music of the cosmos, to which he was attuned, is not systematic. The inner life of a soul is not a linear; it crescendos, flowing in waves and echoes, always mysterious. And so we are left with the unenviable task of trying to make sense of Rav Kook's thoughts, prayers, and flashes of insight.

How should we approach the writings of Rav Kook?

Rav Kook is not to be read logically. Analyzing his writings is like scientifically dissecting the colors of a rainbow, like scrutinizing the notal composition of Beethoven's symphonies, like writing a diagnostic breakdown of ice cream. Such analysis may be necessary — and on a certain level even helpful — but it utterly fails to capture the essence of the experience. Intellectual analyses can never fully grasp the depth and fascination of spiritual moments. We read Rav Kook in order to evoke our own inner voice, to help us evolve, to attune our hearing to the music of our souls and of the cosmos.

_____

Rav Kook's Eight Diaries offer a glimpse into the most raw and personal reflections of a mystic scholar who wrote about love, fear, and desire from the depths of the soul.

_____

The question is not: "Did you understand what Rav Kook wrote?" but rather: "How did the mystical writings of Rav Kook evoke your own soulful meditations? How did his words vibrate within you?"

In my case, Rav Kook's writings opened my heart and soul. The vibrations from his soul shook me up. They were like keys unlocking something precious concealed within me. They changed me. That was the beginning of this love story.

Many times on my spiritual journey, I have felt lonely. I've felt unseen by rabbis and teachers. They wanted to fill my brain with content; they wanted to make sure that I diligently performed the mitzvot. They wanted me to walk in their prescribed path. For most of my life, I felt too insecure in my Jewish identity to acknowledge the source of my loneliness. I thought I was the problem, that something was wrong with me. Judaism seemed to be working for others, for my friends and colleagues. Finally, at a breaking point, I went to a very wise rabbi and lamented my predicament. He offered me priceless words of comfort. He said to me, "You are lonely, but you are not alone. Seek out kindred spirits".

When I encountered the first lines of Rav Kook's introduction to the prayer book, I realized that I had finally found a kindred spirit. Rav Kook writes of the unique authenticity of each person's inner voice. He speaks of how one who fails to listen to the voice of his soul suffers from the burden of "toxic stones around one's heart". In a moment, I sensed the "toxic stones" around my own heart slipping away. For the first time, I felt seen.

Throughout his Eight Diaries, one word in particular stands out and continually resonated with me. That word is love. It was interwoven throughout countless entries, as if his whole opus of work was a variation on a singular theme. Whatever odyssey Rav Kook's soul took, he kept coming back to the same word: love.

There are innumerable self-help books about how to find your inner love, how to become a person worthy of love. But we don't talk enough about how we can become more loving human beings.

Love

When Rav Kook talks about love, he enters into a never-ending, relentless, and rhapsodic flow of words. Love kindles his poetic voice. He writes sentences of fifty, seventy-five, even one hundred words without commas or punctuation. When the chord of love is plucked in his soul, he gushes uncontrollably, ecstatically, endlessly. For Rav Kook, love was the major theme of the heavenly music.

Today, there is a lot of talk about emotional intelligence. There are innumerable self-help books about how to find your inner love, how to become a person worthy of love, and how to sustain a loving relationship. Perhaps more than anything else in the world, we want to be loved. Yet I am not sure we talk enough about how we can — and need — to *give* love, how we can become *more* loving human beings.

No one ever told me of the need to grow in my loving. I was utterly unaware that loving is like a muscle that needs to be stretched and developed.

No one ever told me that loving is more than an emotional experience. The scope of my loving had been limited to particular relationships, and dependent on some magical "chemistry". I never even imagined that I could — or that it might be important — to love people outside of my family and circle of friends. I never imagined that I might love people where there wasn't an emotional high, or as my students would say, "sparkage".

Rav Kook taught me that loving is primarily a spiritual experience. It flows from our souls. Or more exactly, it flows from the Source of the universe *into* and *through* our souls. *We channel divine love.*

Rav Kook saw love as the major theme of the heavenly music.

So this is a book about loving. A love story. A guide to loving. A book about how to open ourselves to the teachings of Rav Kook and expand our inner lives to become more loving people. A book about taking the next steps in our giving love.

This is a book about how to open ourselves to the teachings of Rav Kook and expand our inner lives to become more loving people.

Loving Soulfully

All of the Torah — ethics, mitzvot, learning, and practice —
come to remove the obstacles that prevent an
all-encompassing love from expanding and spreading
to every corner of life, everywhere.

Lovesick

Ithr was one single sentence of Rav Kook that turned my life
upside down:

*All of the Torah — ethics, mitzvot, learning, and practice —
come to remove the obstacles that prevent an
all-encompassing love from expanding and spreading
to every corner of life, everywhere.*

Yearning to Grow

How can I become more receptive
to what I am about to learn?

SHK 3:267

No one ever told me that loving was central to living a Jewish life.
I had to wait until I was well into my sixties before I heard about the
aspiration of expanding our love.

Rav Kook utterly shook me up. He redirected my focus to what it
means to be a Jew.

I had always thought that Judaism was about learning Torah, performing good deeds, leading an ethical life, and perhaps growing
spiritually. Family, community, connection to the Jewish People
and the land of Israel were primary themes. Now along comes Rav
Kook and declares that all of these worthy practices and core beliefs
are not the *goals* of Judaism but actually the means! They came to
"remove the obstacles". They are steps and pathways toward a higher

goal. They are all channels leading to a very different objective — to becoming a more loving human being.

Suddenly I felt as if I had been driving for years, driving and driving, but had put the wrong destination into my GPS. My Jewish journey was way off. I had to completely recalibrate where I was going.

Why hadn't anyone told me this before? Why had none of my Jewish teachers, professors, and rabbis ever mentioned to me that Judaism was about loving? Why did I have to wait so long to hear Rav Kook reveal this secret?

I grew up in a marginally connected Jewish home. I went to Sunday school, had a bar mitzvah, and even stayed involved with my synagogue during some of my high school years. Often, I heard that I should strive to be a "mensch," that I should engage in *tikkun olam* (fixing the world). But loving? No one even mentioned the word loving.

I took Jewish Studies courses in college. We talked a lot about anti-Semitism. No professor ever declared, directly or indirectly, that Judaism was about becoming a more loving human being.

When I came to Israel and learned Hebrew at the age of twenty-three, a whole new world opened up for me. I spent almost ten years in yeshiva studying full time: Torah, Gemara, Jewish law, Jewish ethics, prayer, interpersonal relations, and more. I had the privilege to be in the presence of great rabbis. But no rabbi ever talked about becoming a loving person. No one ever set that as a foundational religious aspiration.

I don't remember a rabbi ever talking personally about love. Not in any class, *dvar Torah*, or personal conversation. Rabbis may have offered astute observations on the verse "You shall love your fellow person like yourself" (Leviticus 18:18), but it always seemed to me that their main emphasis was on learning Torah, performing mitzvot, and addressing pressing communal social needs.

> Rav Kook declares that all of the practices and core beliefs are not the goals of Judaism but the means! They came to "remove the obstacles". They are all channels leading to becoming a more loving human being.

After many years of study, I took the examinations to become a rabbi. There was not a single question on my rabbinical exams about love. Nothing close. Nothing about loving God, people, or even myself. Love was totally irrelevant. Totally absent. How could it possibly be that I could become an educational figure, a public Jewish leader, and perhaps even a role model, while being so utterly oblivious to this goal that Rav Kook considered to be central to all of Jewish living?

I learned about loving from my family, and from my high school and college friends. My parents were married for over 60 years, and maintained an adorable romance filled with sentimental gestures. My mother has a sweet tooth, and my father would hide Mr. Goodbar chocolates (her favorite) in various drawers around the house. My college roommate, Brad from New Orleans, was the first person who ever said "I love you" to me. The southern Baptist chaplain at Vassar spoke a lot about love and being loved, especially about loving those who were less fortunate. It was the '70s and love was in the air; we all desperately wanted to be in love.

But in my Jewish world, talk of love was noticeably absent.

Until I encountered Rav Kook.

When I read the writings of Rav Kook, I felt gut-punched, the air knocked out of me, the whole carpet of Judaism swept out from under my feet. I knew there were tons of ideas and subjects I still needed to learn. I was fully aware that there were countless books on the Jewish shelf that I had never opened, and endless realms of knowledge in our three-thousand-year history with which I was barely familiar. But how was it possible for me to miss the main point, the goal and objective of everything?

Rav Kook's words continued to upend my world:

> *I love all. I cannot not love all people, all nations.*

SHK 2:76

> When, after many years of study, I took the examinations to become a rabbi, there was not a single question on my rabbinical exams about love.

Rav Kook's love poured out of him: his love for all of creation, all creatures, and every cell of creation. He loved all people. Unconditionally.

SHK 3:222

When I read those words, I felt an inner shattering — something inside me broke and opened up. Walls I had never been consciously aware of came crashing down. I felt a glimmer of inner blossoming, something new emerging.

"Ani ohev et hakol" Rav Kook wrote — "I love all." What is this *ahava* that Rav Kook is continually writing about? *Ahava* can be translated in English as either "like" or "love." Perhaps it would have been less daunting to translate it as "like." "Like" seems much more doable. Maybe I can achieve "liking" everyone and everything. I work on tolerating people, and from that starting point, liking "all people, all nations" doesn't seem to be such a huge leap.

But "like" is not really in the spirit of Rav Kook. He writes from the depths of his soul: *"Ani cholleh ahava"* — I am lovesick. Could *"Ani cholle ahava"* be "I am like-sick"? I have never heard someone say, "I am 'like-sick'". Rav Kook is *cholle ahava* — lovesick.

In my engagement with Judaism, I had never come across a rabbi who spoke with such raw vulnerability and compassion, such personal integrity and uncensored openness from his soul.

Rav Kook's love poured out of him: his love for all of creation, all creatures, and every cell of creation; his love for God, the Jewish People, those who were aligned with his spiritual vision and those who fought against it. He loved all people. Unconditionally.

Something within me quivered profoundly when I encountered his words: "I love all. I cannot *not* love all people, all nations". I had no idea where these words would lead me. I had no idea even why I wanted to be led. All I knew was that I desperately needed to enter into Rav Kook's world of Judaism and love.

Wandering Freely

What spark in these writings of Rav Kook resonates with you?

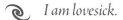 *All of the Torah, Jewish ethics, mitzvot, behavior and actions, Talmudic and spiritual learning, come to remove the obstacles that prevent an all-encompassing love from expanding and spreading to every corner of life, everywhere.*

I love all. I cannot not love all people, all nations.

I am lovesick.

Connecting to our Lives

☑ *On a 1-10 scale of loving, what number would you give to yourself? Why did you give yourself that number?*

☑ *What would be different about your life if you were on a higher number?*

☑ *What obstacles stand in your way to becoming a more loving human being?*

☑ *What steps would you take to overcome these obstacles?*

The Wisdom
of the Soul

W hat does Rav Kook mean when he writes of "an all-encompassing love ... expanding and spreading to every corner of life, everywhere"?

Yearning to Grow

What small step could I take to deepen my love for all other human beings?

How is this even possible? How is it possible to love *everything?*

I have a hard enough time loving my family, my friends, and those closest to me. I have better days and worse days, and many days when I do not even love myself. So how am I supposed to have "an all-encompassing love" that spreads to everything, everywhere, all the time? It seems completely unrealistic, Pollyanna-ish. Yet Rav Kook lived very much in this world. He was known not only for writing about love but also for living a life of love. His contemporaries reacted in astonishment when he responded with love to the rabbis and public figures who continually — and sometimes brutally — defamed him. For this Jewish mystic, there was no other way.

How did he do it? How was it possible?

For Rav Kook, the act of loving was not, at its source, an emotional experience. Loving is expressed emotionally, but not based on emotion.

Love, as an emotion, vacillates. It is unpredictable. We fall in and out of love. We cannot regulate the depth or timing of an emotion. Emotions come in cycles, wavering endlessly, continually surging and ceasing, arising and abating. It is impossible for an emotion to be fixed or steady. Emotions are not controllable. This is part of their appeal. The beauty of emotions lies in their spontaneity. They are unrestrained and sometimes overwhelmingly powerful. It is impossible for us to feel the same emotion constantly toward any one person, for all people, for all things, for all time. It is impossible to sustain an emotion of love forever.

Moreover, love as a purely emotional experience is restrictive. It is limited to the people we want to be with. Even if we *decide* to love everyone, we cannot necessarily *feel* it. We know intuitively when someone is artificially simulating love. We certainly cannot decide to arouse our emotions for everyone and everything, all of the time. Love as an emotion is dependent on our moods and whatever else is going on in our lives.

Even worse, love as an emotion can be potentially damaging and dangerous. It can engender hatred, anger, and jealousy. I may love my children so much that I become jealous of the neighbor's children and secretly want them not to succeed. In my heart, I may come to despise their successes. I may become resentful of their qualities or achievements and be provoked to gossip about them or withhold assistance from them when they need it. When love manifests itself purely as an emotional experience, it can prompt socially destructive behavior.

Additionally, sometimes the emotion of love can be selfish and self-serving. It can be all about me, about my experience of loving. Is my loving for myself or for the other person? The emotion of love can make me feel good. It can restore and heighten my feelings of self-worth. It can help me escape my existential loneliness. It can

---

Love as a purely emotional experience is restrictive. It is limited to the people we want to be with.

---

bring meaning and excitement into my life. Love can be more about the person loving than the person being loved.

When I say "I love you," is the emphasis more on the "I" or on the "you"? If when I say, "I love you," it makes me feel excited, vulnerable, perhaps even edgy, then it probably has more to do with my experience than with the actual love for the other person. When saying "I love you" is thrilling, passionate, and full of sparks, then it is probably reflective of what is going on within me.

Loving seems so difficult and tricky. Rav Kook seems to be setting the bar too high — "an all-encompassing love, expanding and spreading, to every corner of life, everywhere".

For Rav Kook, loving is not grounded in emotion. The source of love is not my heart. The source of love is my soul.

According to Rav Kook, loving is an unconditional expression of our inner being. It flows naturally from our soul. When we are fully aligned with our soul, our loving naturally bursts out. For Rav Kook, the spiritual human being is a loving human being. Love does not depend on a mood or a temperament or a state of mind. It is not personality-based or contingent on what is going on with me or others.

> *I have no need whatsoever*
> *to force this feeling of love.*
> *It flows straight from the depth*
> *of the wisdom of the soul.*

"Love flows naturally from one's soul"! *Wow!* This insight of Rav Kook exploded within me. It utterly shattered my understanding of love, my experience of loving. Love is more than falling in love? More than "chemistry" and "sparkage"? Loving is not limited to how I feel?

What is this "wisdom of the soul" from which, according to Rav Kook, love flows?

When I say "I love you," is the emphasis more on the "I" or on the "you"?

SHK 2:76

29

"Wisdom" (in Hebrew: *chachma*), in the Jewish mystical world, is qualitatively different from knowledge, intelligence, or erudition. It does not stem from rational understanding, analysis, or logical comprehension. Nor does it emerge from our mental capacity. Rather, like intuition, it comes to us from above, from the transcendent. Wisdom is not generated by our minds. It is *received* — a moment of truth and clarity that enters us. Wisdom is the awareness of the eternal, of God's ways. It is a window into the beyond, the spiritual, the mysterious.

The "Wisdom of the soul" is the soul's mystical message, which is always speaking to us. If we were to ask the soul to put its message into words, it would be something like: "Be a force of oneness in this beautiful and broken world. Be a force of love. Love him, love her, love it, love them. God has brought you into this world to manifest your capacity of endless loving."

Our *feelings* of love *express* and *manifest* this inner drive of the soul.

Just as blood flows from our heart, so too love flows from our soul. Just as our heart naturally circulates blood throughout our body, so too our soul naturally streams love throughout our life. As bizarre as this may sound, loving is our most pure and natural state of being.

> *Love for humanity should burst forth —*
> *as a natural inner flowing*
> *from the source of kindness —*
> *not as something commanded,*
> *for then*
> *it would lose*
> *its most luminous quality.*

Rav Kook believed that God hardwires us to love, to be forces of love and connection in the world. We don't *learn how* to love. It is our nature. Rav Kook continually refers to love as "bursting forth". It is

---

Just as blood flows from our heart, so too love flows from our soul.

SHK 1:564

---

not quiet, shy, or gentle. It is a powerful inner force which courses through us, wave upon wave, gushing and surging, impossible to pause or halt. Love is an expression of our souls. We shouldn't plan it, overthink it, organize it, or deliberate over it. And while Rav Kook certainly valued the worthiness of following commands, he beseeched his own soul not to look at loving as an obligation, as something we do because we are being commanded to love others. We need merely to remove the obstacles to allow for it to flow forth. It's our spiritual DNA, hardwired into our very being.

This was a hard idea for me to digest: "Love for humanity should burst forth". I'm not a "burst forth" kind of guy. My mother is from Vienna and our family is more of a "don't let things get out of control" mindset. We weren't big on spontaneity. We excelled at inhibition. When I let it all hang out and go wild, I play chess!

What does it mean to be "hardwired to love"?

Rav Kook writes,

> *The Supreme Holiness (God)*
> *is full of love, kindness, and compassion,*
> *stemming from its abundant and exquisite*
> *wholeness and oneness.*

In other words, "Love, kindness, and compassion" are *continually flowing from God.*

We often declare that God is one. Perhaps the most well-known line in the Torah and the prayer book is the Shema: "Hear Israel, the Lord Our God, the Lord is One." The last word, "*echad,*" is usually translated as "one". That is, the cardinal number one, in contrast to two or three or four. But perhaps a better translation would be not "one" but "oneness." God is ultimate oneness.

What does Oneness do? Oneness does oneness.

Love is an expression of our souls. We shouldn't plan it, overthink it, organize it, or deliberate over it.

SHK 1:346

Oneness emanates oneness. Oneness spreads oneness. Oneness radiates and exudes oneness. Oneness is not a state of being, but rather a pulsating force in the universe. Oneness creates more oneness, more unity, more harmony, more unison. God's oneness is the power urging all things to move toward a state of greater oneness, of greater togetherness and solidarity. For Rav Kook, God is not merely a distant spiritual entity, disconnected from the flow of this world. Yes, God is transcendent and beyond. But God is also a numinous dimension in this world, immanent within every cell of creation. This Godly dimension drives all created beings to be themselves forces of oneness.

Just as the physical force of gravity pulls all things toward the center of Earth, so too, writes Rav Kook, the spiritual force of oneness pulls all beings toward more oneness in the world. This force of God's oneness beats within each of us — in our souls and in the soul of every cell of creation. The driving force in the world — God's will — is also our will. As Rav Kook writes, "The will of a human being is not an isolated private matter; it is a piece of God and stems from the holy divine will, which is continually creating the universe." (SHK 8:77).

What do we call this force of unifying oneness, urging and driving all beings to greater unity? We call it love! Love is the unifying force in the world. Love is what brings everyone and everything together. Love engenders greater oneness.

And now we can understand how we are hardwired to love. In grade school we learned that if A equals B, and if B equals C, then A equals C.

So too, if A — God, the source of oneness, is the driving force bringing about greater oneness in the world, and B — we are created in the image of God, then C — we too are driven to bring about more oneness in the world.

Oneness is not a state of being, but rather a pulsating force in the universe.
What do we call this force urging and driving all beings to greater unity? We call it love!

How do we do bring about more oneness? Through loving. Our souls are forces of love in this world.

Rav Kook writes,

> *Who can stop the light of divine love*
> *that pulsates in the heart?*

SHK 3:267

Love is pulsating within us. Our soul is always calling to us, whispering to us, singing to us: "Be a force of oneness. Bring separate pieces together. Harmonize disparate parts. Be a force of connection. Be the energy of love". Loving is not only a nice act, a warm or pleasant experience. Loving is a *soulful experience*. When we manifest this divine love vibrating in our souls, when we become forces of oneness in the world, it is at those moments that we are most fully living in the image of God. We are most fully expressing our souls and true nature. We are channeling "the wisdom of the depth of our soul".

And, intuitively, we know this. I once asked a group of teenagers, "When was the last time you felt really good and proud of yourselves?" Not a single one of them spoke about their school or extra-curricular successes. Without exception, they gave examples of generosity, of doing something for someone else — of expressing love.

Another time, a former student made aliyah to Israel and took great care to set up a beautiful apartment. A few years later she decided to return to the US. Before she left, she approached me with a perplexed look on her face. "Explain this to me," she said. "Why am I getting so much more pleasure out of giving away my furniture and gadgets than when I bought them for myself?" The answer is that acting in alignment with our nature brings about its own good feeling. Loving is its own reward.

When we allow this love that God has implanted within us to flow outward naturally — loving all creation and all people — we become sanctified. Loving is not only a connection between us and the world,

> When we become forces of oneness in the world, it is at those moments that we are most fully living in the image of God.

it is a connection which brings God, through us, into the world. By bringing this loving energy flowing from God into the world, we sanctify all of creation. We elevate everything and everyone that receives this loving energy flowing through us.

We can now begin to understand the powerful words of Rav Kook:

All of the Torah — ethics, mitzvot, learning, and practice —
come to remove the obstacles that prevent an
all-encompassing love from expanding and spreading
to every corner of life, everywhere.

The drive of love is already within us. We do not need to create or engender love. We do not need to imbibe some kind of love potion. And we certainly do not need to "fall" in love. Our souls are themselves engines of love. Our souls, created in the image of God, are always urging us to become sources of oneness and to bring more unity into the world. Becoming more spiritual, for Rav Kook, always means becoming more loving.

But — and it is a big but — life gets in the way. We learn how not to love. There are countless obstacles that get in the way of our loving — fear, hurt, inhibition, insecurity, rejection, trauma. Life teaches us how to restrain and hold back our love; life manifests obstacles to loving.

Yet God, the source and force of oneness, has not only hardwired us to love, but is beneficently aiding and guiding us to actualize the potential of loving within us. So this God of love, this God of oneness who is continually emanating oneness, gave us the medicine for healing ourselves, for guiding ourselves back to being forces of oneness. To overcome the seemingly insurmountable obstacles that life places in our path, God gave us "All of the Torah — ethics, mitzvot, learning and practice".

Becoming more spiritual, for Rav Kook, always means becoming more loving.

God gave us Judaism. Judaism comes to remove the obstacles to loving so that our natural, hardwired, soulful predisposition to love can emerge, expand, and spread to every person and all of creation.

How can I tell when I am channeling the love of my soul? What are the signs that I am on the right track?

Loving is not just an awareness, a state of mind. Loving cannot remain just "deep wisdom". Loving is an active force. *True loving always leads to action, touching and inspiring the world.*

Unfortunately, becoming a more loving person will not help me sing on-key or improve my sense of humor. My cooking will still be a little bit off, and there's no chance that I will become better looking. But there are two tell-tale signs that some changes are taking place.

The first sign: is my loving affecting me? Do the people around me notice any difference in my character traits, my patience, my openness, my integrity?

> *The telling effects of sacred loving*
> *are the advent of better qualities,*
> *truthfulness, and sincerity,*
> *in even the smallest interactions.*

My loving needs to expand and affect every part of my personality, to impact my intellect, emotions, and actions. I feel healthier, perhaps physically, but certainly in my core self. Rav Kook would say that as I listen more deeply to my inner voice, I become more aligned with God and with the whole universe. This alignment with my true nature is the source of my well-being.

The second sign: is my loving affecting those around me? Soulful love always impacts others. It is a force which vibrates endlessly. It is an engine inside us producing waves and waves of energy which overflow to all who surround us.

Soulful love always
impacts others.

SHK 3:267

SHK 8:54

Loving, in its pure form,
expands to all who have contact with the loving soul.

Anyone who has even incidental contact
with the loving person
is affected and transformed.

SHK 3:267

In Jewish law, to validate a verdict there need to be two witnesses. For soulful loving, there are also two signs: Am I being transformed? Are those around me being transformed?

Wandering Freely

What spark in these writings of Rav Kook resonates with you?

- *I have no need whatsoever to force this feeling of love. It flows straight from the depth of the wisdom of the soul.*

- *Love for humanity should burst forth — as a natural inner flowing from the source of kindness — not as something commanded, for then it would lose its most luminous quality.*

- *Who can stop the light of divine love that pulsates in the heart.*

- *The telling effects of sacred loving are the advent of better qualities, truthfulness, and sincerity, in even the smallest interactions ... Anyone who has even incidental contact with the loving person is affected and transformed.*

- *Loving, in its pure form, expands to all who have contact with the loving soul.*

Connecting to our Lives

- ☑ *Do you sense a spiritual dimension in your connecting with other people?*

- ☑ *Has Judaism helped you become a more loving human being?*

- ☑ *Imagine you had a spiritual x-ray machine which could see through to your soul. You see it bursting with love. How would this image impact you? How do you think it would affect your daily life?*

LOVING GOD

———

It is utterly impossible not to love God.

Loving God

Yearning to Grow

What would be different if I yearned more to live in the presence of God?

SHK 1:696

Rav Kook's love for everything — for all people and for all of creation — originated neither from other people nor from the world. His love for the deep wisdom flowing from his soul did not begin with his love for his soul. It all began with his love for God.

I think this sentence pretty much summarizes Rav Kook's relationship to God:

It is utterly impossible not to love God.

For most of us, not only does it seem absolutely possible not to love God, but also extremely likely for us to live with spiritual doubts and uncertainty. We are probably tempted to ask ourselves: With all the suffering and evil in the world, how could someone love God so much? We do not know if Rav Kook asked himself theological questions during the most difficult periods of his life. He did undergo periods of profound suffering. His first wife died at a very young age shortly after their marriage. His 12-year-old daughter tragically died in an accident. He lived through the horror of World War I. At the end of his life, he endured years of debilitating cancer. Yet we never see that he swayed from his belief that "It is utterly impossible not to love God."

Loving God was Rav Kook's lived reality. From his writings it appears that he was in continual conversation with what he referred to as *"Kodesh Elyon"* (the Transcendent Holiness). This conversation was his ongoing life experience.

For Rav Kook, there was only unqualified, unconditional love. He did not need arguments or proofs. Nor did he express reservations or skeptical thoughts. His personal spiritual experience eradicated doubts and questions. Rav Kook, the mystic, lived in full relationship with the transcendent — with the palpable sense of Oneness and in the presence of holiness. In a sense, he was always blinded by the light of God. He dwelled in the divine palace. He felt and saw holy sparks everywhere — rays of light emanating from the Source of light. He didn't think it, he didn't feel it, he *experienced* it, and he was absorbed in it.

> *Lightning bolt after lightning bolt strike my soul,*
> *Flame after flame inflame my soul.*

When talking about God, Rav Kook was at his most mystical self. He often wrote of the mystery, the impossibility of grasping the holy. He yearned to be absorbed into transcendent reality, which was always present, yet never attainable. He lived in a holy liminal space of "almost". He dwelled in the paradox of an intimate relationship with a being who was always beyond his intellectual, emotional, or even spiritual reach.

> *I am filled with love for God.*
> *I know that what I seek, what I love,*
> *is called by no name.*
> *How can that which is*
> *greater than everything,*
> *greater than goodness,*
> *greater than [any] attribute,*
> *greater than being,*

Rav Kook lived with the paradox of an intimate relationship with a being who was always beyond his intellectual, emotional, or even spiritual reach.

SHK 3:208

be called by any name?
And I love,
and I say: I love God.

SHK 1:164

"And I love, and I say: I love God". "I love God" even though the word "God" is utterly inadequate. Even though the transcendent "is called by no name" and lies beyond all human expression. Even though any word or language is nothing more than a poor translation of experience, and there is no human speech which can capture the dimension of the holy. Even in the face of all this, Rav Kook accepts the conundrum of the human condition and employs the deficient and unsatisfactory term: "God" to describe the source and focus of his love. He lives in holy defiance of his physical and spiritual limitations.

Not only did Rav Kook personally love God, but he believed that the whole cosmos was similarly hard-wired to love the Creator of the world, the source of infinite light.

> *The never-ending desire to be drawn into*
> *the source of pure reality,*
> *the source of infinite light,*
> *is embedded within the entire cosmos,*
> *within all of creation.*
> *This is the fundamental drive which generates*
> *every movement of being,*
> *every moment of development and evolving,*
> *which produces all the drives in the world,*
> *and is the elemental inner force*
> *which propels all human cultures,*
> *all societies, and all nations.*
> *This desire permeates all of creation,*
> *from the tiniest part of the most miniscule beings*
> *to the highest part of the most heavenly angels.*
> *The "desire of desires",*

Rav Kook accepts the conundrum of the human condition and employs the deficient and unsatisfactory term: "God" to describe the source and focus of his love.

the "yearning of yearnings",
is to be absorbed into
the original source of all being,
to be drawn into the being
of the Creator.

SHK 8:160

This quote from Rav Kook's writings deserves to be read again and again and again. It encapsulates his entire approach to life.

Everything is yearning — yearning for the transcendent. The soul, which to various degrees is present in every cell of creation — even in "the tiniest part of the most miniscule being" — is yearning to reunite with the source of all souls. Every cell mystically remembers where it came from and longs to return home. Every cell of creation has within it a desire to turn toward its source. Just as a plant turns toward the sun, the source of light, so too every cell of creation turns toward God, the source of its spiritual light. This is a "never-ending desire".

Rav Kook often writes:

My spiritual desire
to be drawn
into the being of the King
knows no limit.

Rav Kook believed that this unquenchable yearning was the driving force propelling the world to evolve — physically, morally, and spiritually. This desire, "generating every movement of being", brought him great happiness and contributed to his optimistic view of life.

Rav Kook's love for God overpowered and overwhelmed him. Occasionally, he was so taken with this spiritual yearning that before praying he needed to walk outside and calm himself down. In a sense, Rav Kook was saturated through and through with the love of *Kodesh Elyon* (The Highest Holiness).

The soul, which to various degrees is present in every cell of creation — even in "the tiniest part of the most miniscule being" — is yearning to reunite with the source of all souls. Every cell mystically remembers where it came from and longs to return home.

SHK 1:656

This love that "knows no limit" was not only directed toward the Divine. Rav Kook's love for God filled him and spilled over to all who were in his presence, and even those beyond his presence. It led him to "strive to aid all others, all people, and all of the world".

One who continually seeks God,
who feels in one's soul an inner drive
pushing to the light of God,
thirsting for God,
will be fearless and joyous in the gift of this destiny.
This person will know that this holy love
and thirst is not for oneself alone,
but for the whole world,
and at all times
this one will strive to aid all others,
all people,
and all of the world.

SHK 7:208

Wandering Freely

What spark in these writings of Rav Kook resonates with you?

❧ *It is utterly impossible not to love God.*

❧ *I am filled with love for God. I know that what I seek, what I love, is called by no name. How can that which is greater than everything, greater than goodness, greater than [any] attribute, greater than being, be called by any name? And I love, and I say: I love God.*

❧ *The never-ending desire to be drawn into the source of pure reality, the source of infinite light, is embedded within the entire cosmos, within all of creation. This is the fundamental drive which generates every movement of being, every moment of development and evolving, which produces all the drives in the world, and is the elemental inner force which propels all human cultures, all societies, and all nations. This desire permeates all of creation, from the tiniest part of the most miniscule beings to the highest part of the most heavenly angels and transcendent seraphim. The "desire of desires", the "yearning of yearnings", is to be absorbed into the original source of all being, to be drawn into the being of the Creator.*

❧ *One who continually seeks God, who feels in one's soul an inner drive pushing to the light of God, thirsting for God, will be fearless and joyous in the gift of this destiny. This person will know that this holy love and thirst is not for oneself alone, but for the whole world, and at all times this one will strive to aid all others, all people, and all of the world.*

Connecting to our Lives

- ☑ *On a 1-10 scale, how much do you seek to live in the presence of God?*

- ☑ *What would your life be like if you yearned more? What would be different?*

- ☑ *What is holding you back?*

- ☑ *What advice would you give to yourself to increase your connection to the presence of God?*

Waking Up Loving God

What small step could I take to wake up with more positivity, more kindness, and more love?

It is not easy to wake up in the morning. My body is tired; my soul is tired. I wake up reluctant to get out of bed, lingering. Comfortably lying on the mattress, covered by warm blankets, my head on the pillow.

Before I even open my eyes, my mind is whirring with all the things I need to do. I envision the to-do list, as if it were hanging from the ceiling, announcing its presence. It is the first thing I think of in the morning. I'm not even out of bed and I am already feeling overwhelmed; so many demands on my time and energy. I haven't even put my feet on the floor and I am already feeling battered. I am already behind schedule. Anxiety and questions of self-worth begin to settle in. I am dwelling in dread.

What a horrible way to start the day.

The Hasidic Masters said that the way we begin our day represents its spiritual conception. Every day a new day is born. My first thoughts continue to accompany me throughout the day. I open the door to let them in, and then they escort me all day long, even and often against my will. The mood and energy of the day is set at its very first moment. The first thoughts of the day conceive its DNA, which will shape and influence how it progresses.

When my first thoughts of the day circle around my to-do list, my anxiety, and questions of self-worth, it is not surprising that the ensuing day will be less than optimal.

Rav Kook envisions a radically different way to start the day. He sees a day beginning with a loving soulful caress from the Source of compassionate holiness.

Centuries ago in Tzfat, the Hasidic Masters instituted the first line to say upon waking up, consisting of a mere twelve words in Hebrew:

מוֹדֶה (מוֹדָה) אֲנִי לְפָנֶיךָ,
מֶלֶךְ חַי וְקַיָּים,
שֶׁהֶחֱזַרְתָּ בִּי נִשְׁמָתִי,
בְּחֶמְלָה,
רַבָּה אֱמוּנָתֶךָ

Thankful am I for your closeness,
living and sustaining King,
Who returns to me my soul,
compassionately,
great is Your trust.

Significantly, the first word uttered in the morning is not "I". The first word is *modeh/modah*, "thanks". *"Modeh"* precedes *"ani"* ("I") in grammatically questionable form, to make a powerful point. I can't start the day with "I". The first words said in the morning are not "I thank" but "thankful am I". The first thing a Jew thinks about in the morning is not him or herself; not focusing on "me", but rather, on thankfulness. We start our day with gratitude.

This gratitude has many layers, but it's important to note that it's not merely gratitude for the gift of renewed life, for my waking

> The first thing a Jew thinks about in the morning is not him or herself; not focusing on "me", but rather, on thankfulness. We start our day with gratitude.

50

consciousness. Rather, the focus is on the Giver of this supreme gift of life. The first moment of gratitude in the morning is *gratitude for a relationship.*

Rav Kook unpacks these 3 words — מוֹדֶה (מוֹדָה) אֲנִי לְפָנֶיךָ — Thankful am I for your closeness:

> *The first display for the elation of life,*
> *brings with it the highest transcendent ecstasy,*
> *which is expressed by giving thanks.*
> *With the first ray of holiness…*
> *the human being finds itself*
> *in the presence of God,*
> *and in deep love,*
> *with the sweetness of sacred friendship*
> *and the boldness of entering the Holy of Holies,*
> *audaciously pronouncing the word:*
> *"L'fanecha" (Your closeness).*

We begin our day not overwrought with obligations and stuff to accomplish, not drowning in our to-do list. We enter the moment of waking up in "elation of life, transcendent ecstasy, and gratitude". Even though we do it every day, the moment of waking up should never become routine. It is as if we are witnessing our own physical birth; it is as if we re-experience God blowing a soul into our body. It is a moment worthy of ecstasy.

Rav Kook continues to expand these three words. We are not just grateful for being in the presence of God, we are, in fact, close to God, "*l'fanecha*". Rav Kook describes this closeness as the "sweetness of sacred friendship".

The tenth word of this opening line "בְּחֶמְלָה," "compassionately", reinforces this sacred friendship with God. God not only returns my soul to me, God returns my soul to me — "compassionately".

The first moment of gratitude in the morning is gratitude for a relationship.

Commentary on the prayer book

Rav Kook comments:

The quality of divine compassion
bestows itself on the soul,
as it confers compassion
on the devitalized body,
lying bereft of life or light.
And with this divine compassion,
she (the soul) continues to give light to the body,
to restore it with flowing life.

My day is conceived with "the sweetness of sacred friendship". I awaken feeling drenched with the compassion of God. I awaken "in deep love".

Imagine how it would feel to wake up each morning with our first sensory glimpse of the world being: "I am loved. God believes in me enough to return my soul to me. I am the recipient of the compassion of God. I am beloved".

My wife Sandra suggested that this "sweet, loving expression of sacred divine compassion" is really a heavenly caress, a spiritual kiss. Now we both begin our day by slowly caressing our cheeks and saying: מוֹדֶה (מוֹדָה) אֲנִי לְפָנֶיךָ (Thankful am I for Your closeness). Heavenly compassion. The dawning of a new day begins with God's kindness and love.

The first thing on my to-do list is now something new: to pass it forward, to pass God's love, God's "sweetness of sacred friendship" forward. To channel this compassion, this heavenly caress, this divine love — and bring it into the world. To continually wake up, again and again, feeling beloved, throughout the day.

The day's aspiration is to keep repeating "*Modeh ani*" during the day, and each time to feel the gift of a heavenly caress.

The dawning of
a new day begins with
God's kindness and love.

Wandering Freely

What spark in these writings of Rav Kook resonates with you?

- *With the first ray of holiness ... the human being finds itself in the presence of God, and in deep love, with the sweetness of sacred friendship.*

- *The quality of divine compassion bestows itself on the soul.*

Connecting to our Lives

- ☑ *What are the first thoughts you think and words you say as you wake up? What advice would you give to yourself to bring more loving into your morning routine?*

- ☑ *When you get dressed, think about the countless number of people who were involved to design, make, and transport your clothing to you for this moment. Express gratitude and love for them.*

- ☑ *The first time you look into the mirror - smile at yourself.*

- ☑ *Change one piece of your morning routine.*

LOVING THE WORLD

It is impossible not to be full of love for all of creation,
as the beauty of God's light shines in it,
and everything reveals God's kindness,
which fills the earth.

Loving Rocks
and Sand

It doesn't seem like there's much to love about rocks or stones or sand. Or water or stars, or any other inanimate object.

They don't talk. They don't express emotions. They don't choose where to live or when to move.

When I walk on the beach, I don't notice any particular grain of sand more than another. They all seem the same to me. There is no grain of sand that attracts my attention, that welcomes me into a relationship.

The poet William Blake might have been able to "see the world in a grain of sand" but it doesn't seem to me there is much potential for any kind of connection with a tiny bit of earth. Not much chance of getting to know one another!

But that was not the case for Rav Kook.

*The inanimate,
which appears to be still and quiet,
is really full of countless movements
and perpetual motion,
at every moment,*

Yearning to Grow

What would happen if I sensed that every cell of creation had a divine soul?

57

SHK 4:66

even in its most infinitesimal parts,
which continually vibrate.

Sand, rocks, and stones only appear to be inert. They don't appear to us to be moving. But for Rav Kook, they were continually vibrating. Not only were they vibrating, they were also, in their own way, calling to God.

Even the inanimate has within it
the power of grasping the divine.

SHK 1:845

According to Rav Kook, none of us can really ever grasp the divine. None of us has the wisdom, power, or capacity to comprehend the transcendent dimension of life. So, in that regard, we are not qualitatively different from the stones or rocks. We are all physical beings, incapable of figuring out the otherworldly. And yet, both humans and the inanimate have within us a spiritual presence that is yearning to return to its source, to become one with the Creator of the physical world. This spiritual presence is continually vibrating, yearning to return to its original oneness. Every cell of creation possesses a mystical memory, remembering where it came from. Every cell of creation is inviting our consciousness to connect to oneness; every cell is a portal to the sacred, inviting us to be transported to greater awareness of the presence of God.

Rav Kook saw everything in the world as having both a body and a soul. Even a grain of sand.

We need to see the soul of things.
The world in general,
every person and every living thing,
every plant and every inanimate thing,
every star and every sky,
every river and every sea,
every vision and every movement,

Rav Kook saw everything in the world as having both a body and a soul. Even a grain of sand.

---

all exist in the splendor
of their spiritual soulfulness.

SHK 4:76

If every grain of sand has a "spiritual soulfulness", how could I not love it?

Every particle of creation, every cell of being, has within it "the splendor of spiritual soulfulness." A spark of God's transcendent light animates even the inanimate. We can, as William Blake suggests, "hold Infinity in the palm of our hands."

So I decided I would try to experiment with this idea and love something very small and inanimate. I would strive to love...dust.

For some unfathomable and mysterious reason, God brings dust into the world. It doesn't seem to me to be of much help or contribute much. I sweep the dust off the bookshelves, off the table, out of the house, and God brings it back. It always comes back. As if to say, "I am here. You will never get rid of me. Notice me, see me".

How is it possible to love dust? We would be happy to pay someone to get rid of the dust in our houses. I don't know what it is, why it is, or what purpose it serves. It's just a speck of something. Does it deserve to be loved? Is there God's light in the dust? There are specks of dust everywhere. What would happen if I noticed the dust and loved a few specks today? Can I expand my love to include a particle of dust?

So I tried for a while to be in relationship with dust. I watched it. I tried to imagine the particles inside of it moving. I followed it as it was blown from place to place. I wanted to relate to it.

I can't say my experiment was a roaring success. I somehow failed to develop a deep, flowing love of oneness in the specks of dust. But I did notice it, and come to value its existence. Something I had never appreciated before. A small step.

Every particle of creation, every cell of being, has within it "the splendor of spiritual soulfulness."

Bezalel Naor, a serious scholar of Rav Kook's writings, once asked Rav Kook's son, Rav Zvi Yehuda Kook, then in his 80's, "How much did your father love the Jewish People?" Rav Zvi Yehuda leaned back in his chair and began to laugh uncontrollably. He finally replied to Bezalel, "How much did my father love the Jewish People?! My father loved the chair you are sitting on. My father loved the floor your feet are on. My father loved the plant on this desk. My father loved everything. That is how he lived".

"My father loved everything. That is how he lived". Rav Kook saw nothing as ordinary, nothing was bereft of God's light, unworthy of God's love.

For Rav Kook the question was: "How could one not love the inanimate — pebbles, stones, rocks, and sand"?

Nature was the revealed expression of the miraculous. For Rav Kook, the natural and the supernatural were intrinsically entwined. Like night and day, they formed one indivisible entity.

*The miraculous and the natural are one unit;
the miraculous is nature's inner soul.*

It's easy not to pay attention to something that seemingly has no life. An extraordinary act of nature — a tornado, a flood, or a double rainbow — naturally catch our attention. But otherwise it seems like nature is just doing its thing, day in, day out, year after year. Hardly noteworthy.

But what happens when we begin to sense that what is seemingly ordinary is actually an expression of the divine?

What happens when we begin to sense that there is a spiritual presence, a soulfulness, in everything?

What happens when we take a walk and notice not only the seemingly mundane presence of nature, but also its radiant beauty ?

What happens then? What happens when we begin to sense that we live in a sacred world?

According to Rav Kook, that is when we begin to fall in love with the world.

> *The recognition that the whole world,*
> *in all of its countless expressions,*
> *is only divine radiant light clothed in various coverings,*
> *implants in one's heart a love of unequivocal truth.*
> *It is impossible not to be full of love for all of creation,*
> *as the beauty of God's light shines in it,*
> *and everything reveals God's kindness,*
> *which fills the earth.*

SHK 8:57, 1:696

Wandering Freely

What spark in these writings of Rav Kook resonates with you?

- *The inanimate, which appears to be still and quiet, is really full of countless movements and perpetual motion, at every moment, even in its most infinitesimal parts, which continually vibrate.*

- *Even the inanimate has within it — the power of grasping the divine.*

- *We need to see the soul of things. The world in general, every person and every living thing, every plant and every inanimate thing, every star and every sky, every river and every sea, every vision and every movement, all exist in the splendor of their spiritual soulfulness.*

- *The miraculous and the natural are one unit; the miraculous is nature's inner soul.*

- *The recognition that the whole world, in all of its countless expressions, is only divine radiant light clothed in various coverings, implants in one's heart a love of unequivocal truth. It is impossible not to be full of love for all of creation, as the beauty of God's light shines in it, and everything reveals God's kindness, which fills the earth.*

Connecting to our Lives

☑ Walk outside. Find a comfortable place to sit quietly. Select one item — inanimate or natural. Look at it for at least one minute. Then imagine this object communicating to you. It begins by saying: "I'm so glad you chose me. This is what I would like to say to you...." Finish its words.

☑ Write your response to this object.

Loving Flowers
and Trees

Yearning to Grow

How can I come to appreciate all
of nature, even the features that I
wouldn't usually notice?

Everyone loves flowers. What's not to love? Roses. Tulips. Cro-
cuses. Is there anything more stunning than a blue iris? Is there
a better smell in all the world than a hyacinth? I want to grab every
moment of the dramatic twenty-four-hour bloom of a hibiscus flower.

But do we love the flowers themselves or do we love the pleasure they
give us? And is it the whole plant that we love, or merely its most
colorful and glamorous parts?

Usually, our attention is drawn only to the flashy bit of the plant,
its blossom. Flowers can be magnificent, even magical. As I write
this, the purple bougainvillea in our front yard is climbing up our
jacaranda tree. The bright purple of the bougainvillea against the
pale purple of the jacaranda is breathtaking, purple on purple. I
could look at it all day.

But what am I not seeing? What is escaping my attention? What
am I not noticing?

I'm not really paying any attention to the branches of the bougainvillea
or the trunk of the jacaranda. I certainly haven't thought about their
roots at all. It's easy for me to overlook the leaves, especially the leaves

that are beginning to turn brown. Those are just a distraction from the eye-catching shades of purple. That is really all I notice.

So do I actually love the tree and the whole flower, or do I love only the tiny piece of them that attracts me? Am I loving every cell of the tree or the bush? Or have I selected a few of their most glamorous cells that satisfy some personal desire to receive pleasure from my environment? *Is this moment about the flowers and the tree or is it about me?*

Rav Kook would say that focusing only on the flower's beautiful colors is a self-centered and myopic view of nature. Unfortunately, it is probably unavoidable; it is how we instinctively function. But it is not ideal. In fact, it is very far from the ideal. It is a self-serving form of loving. I don't really love the whole being of the bush or the flower or the tree. Rather, I love how I feel when I experience their beauty, when I receive something from them.

This kind of love is all about me. It is certainly not the apprehension of God's light in each and every cell of the flower, bush, or tree. It is certainly not a complete relationship. I am not focusing my full attention on the beloved as a whole, but only on those aspects that give me pleasure. There is no sense — or a very limited sense — of oneness here.

But Rav Kook would generously assuage my guilty feelings and say that it's not really all my fault. The natural world pushes me to focus on final products and not on processes. It is natural that I look at the flower and not at the roots or the stem. That is just how the world works. Nature does not push me to sense God's light in each and every cell of the flower, bush, or tree. It does not push me toward a full relationship.

But in the ideal world, if I truly had a loving relationship with each element of nature, then my relationship with a flower or bush or tree

> Do I actually love the tree and the whole flower, or do I love only the tiny piece of them that attracts me?

would *not* dwell exclusively on what it does for me. I would not love only the attention-getting colorful final product. I would not love only what gratifies me. I would also love the trunk of the tree, and the branch that carried the flower. And I certainly would love the roots, without which nothing would grow. If I truly loved nature, then I would have a full and loving relationship with it — all of it. I would love the whole flower, the whole bush, and the whole tree.

Why is this kind of relationship so hard to develop?

Rav Kook writes,

> *The physical world pours all of its energy*
> *into creating the final product.*
> *It doesn't allow for its full inner luster to emerge.*
> *The day will come*
> *when the taste of the tree*
> *will be as sweet as the taste of its fruit.*

"The final product"… which of course, is what we see. We do not see the *full light* of the flower, the bush, or the tree. We see only the *final light*, the light of its finished product.

And in this way the flower, bush, and tree reflect only the prevalent truth in our world: Our pleasure almost always derives from the achievement of a goal, and rarely on the *process* necessary to achieve that goal. This is the reality of our world, writes Rav Kook. It is a tragic truth.

And yet, we devote far more time and energy to the process toward a goal than on the actual moment of achieving the goal. In our educational systems, we spend years and years in the process that culminates in receiving a degree. An expectant mother spends months and months in the process of awaiting the day of birth. Couples spend weeks or months — or sometimes even years — in the process of planning their weddings. But how much do we love the actual

In an ideal world, if I truly had a loving relationship with each element of nature, then my relationship with a flower or bush or tree would not dwell exclusively on what it does for me.

SHK 3:24; Orot HaTeshuvah 6:7

process? Don't we usually see the process as just something that we need to endure in order to get to the final product? Do we really see the beauty in the "roots and stems" of our own work?

Think about our daily to-do lists. To-do lists are all about the product. If we could fully implement Rav Kook's awareness of focusing on the process and not only on the product, then we would write a completely different type of to-do list. It would be a list that includes — and perhaps even celebrates — the processes.

What would our to-do list look like if we loved not only the product but also the process? Maybe it would then look like this:

- ✴ Find God's light while getting dressed.
- ✴ Find God's light while preparing food.
- ✴ Find God's light while waiting in line.
- ✴ Find God's light while driving to work.
- ✴ Find God's light while cleaning up.
- ✴ Find God's light — *now*.

Rav Kook is urging us to become entirely present in the wonder and splendor of the process. He invites us to bring the sweetness of the final product into the process. Only then will we truly be fully engaged with the world. Only then, will we become our full loving selves — loving the process for the sake of the process and not only for what it will eventually yield.

Only then will we be able to love the whole plant and see God's light in every one of its cells.

The world of nature teaches us about growth, about the *process* of becoming. The external outcome is measurable and publicly acknowledged. The process leading up to the final product is private and

What would our to-do list look like if we loved not only the product but also the process?

internal. No one sees or appreciates the work done in preparation for the final result. We don't celebrate the hidden roots of the tree, or the insides of its trunk. Processes are neither publicly noticed nor applauded, but they are essential to the ultimate products, and thus worthy of our love.

Can I discover the sweetness, the taste, the light, and the holiness in the preparation of the product?

Can I love the process too?

Wandering Freely

What spark in this writing of Rav Kook resonates with you?

 The physical world pours all of its energy into creating the final product. It doesn't allow for its full inner luster to emerge. The day will come when the taste of the tree will be as sweet as the taste of its fruit.

Connecting to our Lives

☑ *Visit a plant nursery. Walk around and imbibe the colors and smells. Buy the plant that grabs your eyes.*

☑ *Now take a moment and with intention look at its roots and stem.*

☑ *Place the plant somewhere in your home or garden (depending on the plant's needs), but in a place where you will see it every day. Think of this plant as your "love the process reminder".*

> Processes are neither publicly noticed nor applauded, but they are essential to the ultimate products, and thus worthy of our love.

LOVING HUMANITY

How much does the heart burst to love everything?
To love all of humanity, all action, all creation?

Loving All People

In a sense, Rav Kook worked backwards. He started at the end; his eyes focused on the ultimate full healing of the brokenness of God's world.

He envisioned resplendent unity and harmony. He transcended the brokenness of present reality and foresaw the transpiring of oneness in the end of days. He saw the whole picture, and then worked backwards to see — with exquisite clarity — each and every point of the picture. Each point was now contextualized into the whole picture of place and time.

In one of his most-quoted poems, he wrote:

> There is a person who sings the song of the soul. . .
> There is a person who sings the song of the nation. . .
> [There is a person who] sings the song of humanity. . .

Most of us do not see the whole picture; we dwell on ourselves or on our community. Perhaps some gifted souls expand the scope of their concern to include their nation. We usually focus on the brokenness closest to our situation — whether personal, communal, or national. Each of us responds to our own personal sense of brokenness. Each

Yearning to Grow

Can I imagine, for a moment, loving all of humanity? How does that feel?

SHK 7:112

type of brokenness brings us to a different sense of yearning. Rav Kook felt the brokenness of the whole universe, of all of creation.

He saw the expansion of one's scope of concern as the true measure of a tzaddik (holy person).

> *The great tzaddikim*
> *feel the Oneness*
> *of all of creation*
> *and love all of creation.*

SHK 3:32

This connection to "the Oneness of all creation" deepened his sense of cosmic brokenness. He felt this brokenness in his innermost being. Such brokenness touches us beyond our linear or cognitive thinking. It does not reside in our intellect. We feel it in our bodies and in our souls. One of his contemporary critics, Yosef Chaim Brenner, known for his vilification of Rav Kook, once described him as a "broken soul". Rav Kook responded, "Of course I am a broken soul. Only a stone-hearted person does not feel the brokenness of the world".

Rav Kook's inner brokenness evoked his creative voice. It brought him to poetry, to song. The notes of his brokenness took him to the greatest highs and lows, crescendoing to an ecstatic melancholy.

Rav Kook writes:

> *Inner sorrow is the raw material*
> *for melancholy poets*
> *to wake up their violins,*
> *and for tragic artists*
> *to reveal their creativity.*

Rav Kook's inner brokenness evoked his creative voice.

SHK 1:340

He wrote of many different aspects of brokenness, of individual, familial, communal, and national brokenness. Each of these were discrete parts of the whole. And yet, Rav Kook lived beyond all of these isolated and disconnected points.

Many people consider Rav Kook to be the quintessential Zionist, the sweet singer and ardent lover of the Jewish People. This is of course true. But, at his core — in his soul — Rav Kook was a universalist. He felt the anguish of the universe. He sang the song of all humanity, of all existence. He was in love with wholeness, with the unity and oneness of reality.

> *And there is one whose soul is so all-encompassing*
> *that it expands beyond the limits of the Jewish people.*
> *One sings the song of humanity.*
> *One's spirit ascends and becomes concerned*
> *With the greatness of humankind and its Divine image.*
> *One seeks humanity's ultimate purpose;*
> *One looks forward to its ultimate perfection.*
> *From this source of life,*
> *one draws*
> *all of one's thoughts and insights,*
> *one's ideals and visions.*

In his soul — Rav Kook was a universalist. He felt the anguish of the universe.

SHK 7:112

"One sings the song of humanity ... From this source of life, one draws all of one's thoughts and insights, one's ideals and visions". According to Rav Kook, we cannot understand, appreciate, or philosophically grasp the Oneness of the world. It is simply beyond human comprehension. We can only sing it. Living in this mindset brought Rav Kook to embrace the process toward greater oneness; to love and yearn for ultimate perfection.

> *Great is my love for all creatures, for all reality.*
> *God forbid I should put in my heart*
> *even a tiny speck of animosity for any people.*
> *I feel in my kishkes a great love for all of creation,*
> *and more than that,*
> *for all human beings.*

SHK 8:116

One could perhaps respond cynically: "What's the point of all this pontificating? So what? The reality is that we come into contact with just a few people every day, we have limited circles of connection and relationships. What's the point of being in love with the universe? With all people? What does it matter? What does it accomplish?"

Rav Kook seems never to have asked such questions. His love of all people simply flowed from his soul.

> *How much does the heart burst*
> *to love everything?*
> *To love all of humanity,*
> *all action, all creation?*

His heart was bursting to love, without limitation, without qualification.

Rav Kook's "singing the song of humanity" motivated him to become curious about all other people. He was not threatened by the gifts, talents, or ideas of other nations. Every nation was chosen for a purpose. Their triumphs were not cause for defensiveness. Rather than feel threatened by the gifts of other nations, he was intrigued; he celebrated humanity's diversity. He saw their achievements as signs of their being blessed by God and as invitations to study and learn more about them.

Rav Kook was guided by two "maybe's".

> *One should not immediately reject any opposing opinion,*
> *even if it deeply challenges a tenet of belief,*
> *rather one should dwell on it.*
> *Maybe one did not understand it completely.*
> *Maybe by clarifying the idea more*
> *some truth, holiness, and light will emerge from it.*

SHK 3:20

In "singing the song of humanity" Rav Kook was motivated to become curious about all other people. He was not threatened by the gifts, talents, or ideas of other nations.

SHK 1:684

Two "maybe's"… These are words of great humility. "Some truth, holiness, and light" may come about through an ideology which initially appears to be misguided or false. Rav Kook lived with his arms wide open, fearless and free.

> *Despite the ideological differences*
> *between religions and beliefs,*
> *and despite the divisions*
> *of races and locales,*
> *it is essential to penetrate deeply into the mindsets*
> *of the differences as much as possible,*
> *to study their character and characteristics,*
> *to discover shared qualities*
> *and intensify love for all people.*

SHK 1:593

Rav Kook's two "maybe's" are a paradigm shift compared to how we often regard other opinions and ideologies.

His words threw me for a loop. I've always loved to argue ferociously. Convinced of my point of view, my objectives were to either prove my point or convince the other side of my truth. Forget harmonious cooperation, I wanted to defeat the other side! And so, my conversations often resembled wrestling matches. There were no "maybe's". There was no "singing the song of humanity". There was no aspiration to "intensify love for all people".

Rav Kook's two "maybe's" come from a soul of humility — a soul wondering how any given nation or ideology can bring oneness into the world. A soul wondering where is the light of God in this different and perhaps even opposing way of thought.

Rav Kook reminds us that our hearts are always bursting "to love all of humanity, all action, all creation" — even those opposed to us. Perhaps especially those opposed to us.

Rav Kook's two "maybe's" come from a soul of humility — a soul wondering how any given nation or ideology can bring oneness into the world.

Wandering Freely

What spark in these writings of Rav Kook resonates with you?

🌀 *And there is one whose soul is so all-encompassing that it expands beyond the limits of the Jewish people. One sings the song of humanity. One's spirit ascends and becomes concerned with the greatness of humankind and its Divine image. One seeks humanity's ultimate purpose; One looks forward to its ultimate perfection. From this source of life, one draws all of one's thoughts and insights, one's ideals and visions.*

🌀 *Great is my love for all creatures, for all reality. God forbid I should put in my heart even a tiny speck of animosity for any people. I feel in my kishkes a great love for all of creation, and more than that, for all human beings.*

🌀 *Despite the ideological differences between religions and beliefs, and despite the divisions of varying races and locales, it is essential to seek to deeply penetrate into the mindsets of the differences as much as possible, to study their character and characteristics, to discover shared qualities and fortify love for all people.*

🌀 *How much does the heart burst to love everything? To love all of humanity, all action, all creation?*

🌀 *One should not immediately reject any opposing opinion, even if it deeply challenges a tenet of belief, rather one should dwell on it. Maybe one did not understand it completely. Maybe by clarifying the idea more some truth, holiness, and light will emerge from it.*

Connecting to our Lives

☑ *Read the International pages of the news. Become curious about a story. Search for another article about the same incident.*

☑ *Look at a map of the world. Pick a country that you know nothing about. Try to find something unique about that country..*

☑ *Have you ever thought of yourself as a "Universalist"? How might being a universalist express itself in your life?*

Loving People who are Difficult to Love

As we saw from the conclusion of the last chapter, Rav Kook sets the bar very high:

> *Love should be*
> *with a full heart and soul —*
> *for all people.*

The question immediately comes up: "But how can I love *that* person?"

First of all, Rav Kook is not saying that we need to justify everyone's actions or agree with everyone's opinions. We can disagree and argue with those whose opinions we perceive to be wrong. Other people's attitudes may be highly antithetical to ours. Their behavior may be highly offensive to us, personally or ideologically. We may seriously differ with their positions on vital communal, national, or religious issues.

Yet, Rav Kook would still have us love them — "with a full heart and soul."

Sometimes, I don't like certain people because their actions irritate me. Like the teenage cashier at the grocery store who was talking on

Yearning to Grow

Can I love even people who are annoying and infuriating?

SHK 1:807

her cell phone instead of ringing up my groceries. Like the neighbor who took my reserved parking spot. Like the guy who was talking too loudly in the library.

Sometimes, I don't like certain people because of their political opinions. Like my cousin who voted for the "other" political party. Like my boss who wears his ideological beliefs on the bumper stickers of his car. Like the pompous, self-righteous know-it-all who never gives me a chance to get a word in and most likely would not pay attention to my opinion even if I did get the chance to voice it.

Sometimes, I don't like certain people because of what they did to me personally. Like my best friend forgetting my birthday. Like people gossiping about me. Like the person who abruptly ended our relationship without explanation.

But whatever issues I have with these people — whether personal or ideological — none of this reflects the whole being of the other person. The traits that I find annoying may reflect the person's attitudes, significant character traits, or typical behavior, but these are all discrete parts of the other. They are *details* of the other human being, not their core identity. Their attitudes, character traits, and actions can change substantially over the course of time. The cashier will grow out of the teenage years. My neighbor may sell his car. My friend may remember my next birthday. I can't allow a single — perhaps momentary — aspect of the other person to represent their whole self. Rav Kook urges us to look deeper, beyond all these transitory external details.

In fact, he would say that this is precisely the "deep wisdom" that I need to acquire. I need to perceive the essential soulful being of the other. I need to become aware of their *shoresh haneshama*, the root (or source) of their soul.

Rav Kook writes,

> Whatever issues
> I have with those who annoy
> me — whether personal
> or ideological — none
> of this reflects the whole
> being of the other person.

Everyone is uniquely formed by
the root of their soul.

Midbar Shor 3

Every person needs to know that he or she
is called to serve God
in their own special way,
according to
the root of their soul.

SHK 4:6

The "root of the soul" is the unchanging, essential, unique spiritual genetic structure that everyone receives at the moment of conception. It is the most essential, foundational concept of spiritual life

To understand Rav Kook's approach to love, we must fully grasp his idea of the "root of the soul".

Everyone has a soul, and everyone has a root (or source) of the soul. The soul is the spiritual equivalent of the double helix of DNA. Just as everyone has unique DNA, so too everyone has a unique soul. While our DNA is the source of our physical lives; the soul is the source of our spiritual lives. The soul is the generic, mysterious, transcendent, animating force which gives us life. Everyone has one.

The "root of the soul" is the spiritual equivalent of the unique genetic structure present at the molecular level of our DNA. Just as everyone has a unique genetic structure, so too everyone has a unique "soul root".

This "soul root" is the reason why every individual is needed in the world. Each of us comes into this world to heal a specific need, to unify a specific brokenness, to address a specific trouble. The world is lacking in something and therefore this person, with this particular "root of the soul", came into being to hopefully provide this rectification. The "root of the soul" carries within it the drive, inclinations, and capacities to provide this tikkun (healing). It is really the essential

> To understand Rav Kook's approach to love, we must fully grasp his idea of the "root of the soul". This "soul root" is the reason every individual is needed in the world.

"I-ness" of each individual. It predisposes and guides us toward the specific role we should play in this world.

This soul root is continuously trying to communicate our role and destiny to us through our will, desires, energy, intuition, and consciousness.

This idea of the root of the soul was life-changing for me. My educational path had only informed me about John Locke's idea of *tabula rasa* — that we are born with a "clean slate," that there is nothing in our innate makeup that determines or influences our future behavior. No nature; only nurture. We are the products of our sensory experience, shaped exclusively by the educational and social forces around us. Now along comes Rav Kook, who says that not only are we not a clean slate waiting to be imprinted by the world, but that we are each born with very distinct and unique qualities, predispositions, purposes, and potential destinies. What makes us unique is not merely the experiences we undergo, but the spiritual make-up we receive at the moment of our conception. *We are all chosen!* The moment the soul root enters our being — we become our potential selves.

When we perceive the "soul root" of the other, we become aware that everyone is created in the image of God. Everyone has been bequeathed a soul. No one comes into this world randomly or accidentally. A soul does not enter a body by mistake. Everyone has been chosen by God to bring something unique and essential into this world. Everyone has a path. Furthermore, God is continually sustaining every person's soul and giving them life.

So, who am I not to love this person, the one whom God has intentionally brought into this world for a vital and necessary purpose? This person upon whom God has bestowed a soul root?

I might be mystified about why on earth this person has to be in the world, and what role he or she could possibly be playing, but

> Our soul root is continuously trying to communicate our role and destiny to us through our will, desires, energy, intuition, and consciousness.

Rav Kook would say that God's light is shining through everyone, without exception. My love should be unconditional.

Rav Kook informs us that love is truly seeing the other, seeing the divine light in the other. More than an emotion, *love is a perception, a "deep wisdom"*. Love is seeing the transcendence of God channeled through the other; seeing the uniquely soulful essence of the other and wanting to come closer to it. The moment I sense this unique godliness in other people, then, despite all our conflicts and disagreements, despite any friction or tension, I want to connect to them. I want to come closer to them. I may come to love them with a full heart and soul.

In short, I can aspire to love everyone because God loves everyone. I can love everyone because God has chosen to give them a soul root, a unique path and purpose in this world.

The moment I sense this unique godliness in other people, then, despite any friction or tension, I want to come closer to them. I may come to love them with a full heart and soul.

Wandering Freely

What spark in these writings of Rav Kook resonates with you?

 Love should be with a full-heart and soul — for all people.

 Everyone is uniquely formed by the root of their soul. Every person needs to know that he or she is called to serve God in their own special way, according to the root of their soul.

Connecting to our Lives

☑ *Write down the name of someone who is difficult for you to love. Write a few words about what it is about this person that makes it so challenging to love him/her.*

☑ *Write about what this person brings up within you.*

☑ *Now write about how you feel about yourself when this person brings you to a non-loving mindset. How do you feel about what you just wrote?*

☑ *Seek out this person for a conversation, not to enter into the "issues", but to talk and listen to each other.*

Loving Is Hard Work

E ven though I may be hardwired to love, even though love may be the most natural impulse of my soul, nevertheless, writes Rav Kook:

> *Loving others demands extensive work,*
> *to expand it to the scope it deserves,*
> *to fight against superficiality,*
> *shallow impressions,*
> *and not fully developed awareness.*

It's so easy and yet it's so hard.

Even though Rav Kook would say that he loved everyone with infinite love, he wrote about his struggle and anguish while being with people with whom he could not fully be himself. He wrote about the pain of needing to limit his light as it would overpower most people in his community. His spiritual insights would not be grasped. A reflective philosophical mystic does not mix well in social settings.

On the one hand, loving is easy — because it's one of the few things we are in control of. We don't need to learn a new language or play a new instrument. We don't have to remember a complicated equation in

Yearning to Grow

Who could I love a little bit more?

SHK 1:593

physics or solve a philosophical quandary. All we need to do is allow the love, already present and flowing within us, to enter our lives.

On the other hand, loving is hard — because we desperately want to protect ourselves from being hurt, disappointed, embarrassed, or taken advantage of. We wound easily and deeply.

Halfway through my first year of teaching, I asked my class for feedback. I told them to be completely honest and direct. I told them that I was an adult and could take criticism, that I welcomed their comments. What a mistake! I had totally overestimated my self-confidence and was devastated by their responses. I was much more fragile than I would ever have admitted.

We can be hurt in so many ways.

What if we express a personal thought, share a vulnerable moment, or offer an act of uninhibited generosity, and someone rolls their eyes or shrugs their shoulders?

What if someone makes a cynical comment or judges us unkindly?

What if we open our hearts 100 percent and someone gives us just 70 percent attention in return?

These fears petrify me. How can I let myself go, let down the guards which serve and protect me, and live with a full and flowing heart? What guarantee do I have that I will not be wounded? Do I have the courage to do this?

Continuing to love, despite all these potential hazards, is hard work.

For me, becoming a more loving person is like running a marathon every day. At certain points, I hit a wall; I feel like I can't go anymore. My love tank is empty. I feel small and often disappointed in myself. This "hard work" seems way too hard.

Rav Kook writes that we need to fight against "superficiality and

---

Loving is hard — because we desperately want to protect ourselves from being hurt, disappointed, embarrassed, or taken advantage of. We wound easily and deeply.

shallow impressions". None of us would admit to being "superficial" or "shallow" people, so why should this happen to us? Unfortunately, life can easily evoke the less shining sides of ourselves.

When do we become superficial? What are the shallow impressions that Rav Kook is referring to?

Shallow impressions result from not seeing the whole person. Shallow impressions occur when I look at others only through *my* eyes, through *my* perspective. It's so easy to consider everyone in relation to myself, my needs and my wants. It's so easy to see others and ask myself, "Do I like them? Are they nice to me? Are they people I would like to spend more time with? Do they have any annoying qualities that will get on my nerves? Will this person help me in any way? Will they benefit or advance my interests?" Human eyes are usually narrow eyes, invested in petty personal concerns.

Rav Kook taught me that I need to fight against these natural and persistent inclinations. Looking at others through the perspective of my own eyes will, at best, lead to conditional relationships and, at worst, lead me to judge others harshly and negatively.

Part of the hard work of loving another is acknowledging that we rarely, if ever, see the full picture. We get only a tiny glimpse into who the other person is. We usually don't know much about their childhood. We probably have no idea how their parents raised them, what formative experiences, issues, or traumas they might have endured. According to Jewish mystical thought, we only truly know the other when we are familiar not only with how their parents raised them, but also how their grandparents raised their parents. We would need to take into account three generations to even begin to see underneath a person's actions and behavior. We would need to know how the grandparents impacted the parents who then impacted the children. Only then would we really have a glimpse into the layered personalities of the children. Without such insight, we can see only

> Part of the hard work of loving another is acknowledging that we rarely, if ever, see the full picture.

the surface layer. Our perennial lack of information regarding what has nurtured and shaped other people should soften and humble our judgments. This humbling reality check should impel us to counter the "shallow impressions and not fully developed awareness" that Rav Kook speaks of.

In the absence of so much information and evidence, how can or should we judge others?

> *We need to have compassion for others,*
> *especially when they disappoint us,*
> *to find the positive in them,*
> *to amplify their virtues.*

SHK 3:158

Our perennial lack of
information regarding what
has nurtured and shaped
other people should soften
and humble our judgments.

Rav Kook shakes us up. Precisely during the times when people disappoint us, we should respond with compassion. At the moment of our frustration, we should make an effort to judge them even more kindly, "to find the positive in them and to amplify their virtues". Rav Kook teaches that moments of dissatisfaction and exasperation with others are not a cause for anger or distance. Rather they are invitations for us to become more compassionate and more loving.

Even when someone behaves abhorrently, Rav Kook writes,

> *We should only feel repulsion*
> *for the person's unscrupulous acts,*
> *while still valuing and loving*
> *their being created in the image of God.*

Midot HaRa'aya, Love, 9

The refining of our love demands that we continually refuse to define people by, or equate people with, their actions. The extensive work of loving requires that we constantly remind ourselves that God created those around us, fashioned their personality traits, and unceasingly nourishes their soul. Despite their troublesome behavior, God is relentlessly keeping these people alive in this world. There must be a purpose for their continued existence. This alone demands our love. We need to move out of our smallness and try to imagine how God sees these people.

> It is great, illumining work
> to look at everyone
> with "beautiful eyes,"
> with boundless compassion,
> to emulate "God's eyes,"
> even for the most iniquitous.

SHK 3:158

I think this is one of Rav Kook's most beautiful phrases: "to look at everyone with beautiful eyes... to emulate God's eyes".

What does it mean to see the world with "beautiful eyes", through "God's eyes"?

"Beautiful eyes " or "God's eyes," are expansive. They look beneath the exterior, beyond the motivations and psyche of the other, to reveal what is concealed. Within every human being, entire worlds lay hidden. Rav Kook writes that secreted within each person is a primal light, a spark, waiting to be revealed. This light, the luminosity of their soul, is a good and benevolent light. I need to believe that it's there. I need to seek it out. I need to remind myself of the beauty of their soul.

Rav Kook saw it. He wrote,

> One needs to afflict oneself
> to love human beings...
> one needs to see their beneficial light
> through which the radiance of God
> spreads in the world.

SHK 1:889

Beautiful eyes lead to seeing the radiance of God within other people. Sometimes it is a tortuous path. One needs to "l'yaser et atzmo", to relentlessly push oneself, to seek out the good hidden deeply within

We need to relentlessly push ourselves to seek out the good hidden deeply within each person.

each person. This is the hard work that Rav Kook talks about. It can be annoying and exasperating work. This person is agitating me. Nauseating me. Why should I take the time to go deeper? Why should I bother to work so hard to "get" this annoying person?

Recently, I had an ultrasound for some stomach pain. Afterward, I wrote to the doctor asking for his evaluation. He wrote me back a very brief answer — just a few words. I wrote to him again with a few more questions. Again, he answered very cryptically. I asked him one more question. Then he wrote back: "BTW, should I get paid per email?!?!?!"

I was tempted to write back something snide, like: "Sorry. I thought this was covered by the Hippocratic oath" or, even worse, "You write so tersely that if I paid you by the word, it would only be a couple of shekels."

Then I paused, realizing my answer was quite self-righteous and spiteful. I thought of Rav Kook and began to "afflict myself," thinking, "He might've had a challenging and tiresome day. He's probably underpaid. At least he didn't ignore my emails." I realized that if I did react nastily to him, I would feel badly and guilty about it afterward. I would be disappointed in my pettiness, my childishness. Where was the soulfulness in that? Where were my "beautiful eyes"? I wrote, "Shabbat Shalom and thank you for all your help and wisdom. I really appreciate it. You've calmed me down and I feel more reassured." He concisely responded: "Shabbat Shalom". I considered it a small victory for my soul.

But it isn't only toward others that we must be wary of superficial relationships. We can also act superficially toward ourselves. We can react to our behavior, without pausing and reflecting on the deeper causes and motivations of our actions. We can overlook that we have countless layers and baggage of history bringing us to our present conduct. There are times in our lives when we exhibit a superficial

> It isn't only toward others that we must be wary of superficial relationships. We can also act superficially toward ourselves.

relationship with ourselves, not allowing deeper, more soulful and loving behavior to come out. We have to work hard to see ourselves with "beautiful eyes" too.

I lived this superficial relationship with myself not long ago.

While recovering from COVID, I was surprised and a bit shocked to see how little patience I had. I got annoyed with slow drivers, exasperated waiting in line at the supermarket, and silently infuriated at people taking too long to make a point. Even the noisy play of my grandkids grated on my nerves. I was getting upset all the time and my touchiness was ruining the mood in our home. COVID had sapped a lot of my physical and emotional strength. I couldn't find the energy to be more generous. I was extremely disappointed with myself for not acting with greater love. This disappointment turned into annoyance, which turned into outrage. I couldn't bear to be with myself.

Then I thought of Rav Kook's description of "beautiful eyes", and of how he might advise me to have compassion for myself even when — *especially when* — I was disappointed with myself. Rav Kook's wisdom reminded me to look not only at how I was behaving, but also to reflect and remember how draining COVID can be and not to judge myself so harshly. It's so easy to fall out of love with ourselves.

Rav Kook writes,

> *When one really looks at the good side*
> *of each and every person,*
> *then one falls in love with everyone*
> *with a soulful affection.*

There is a pay-off for our hard work at loving. When we focus on the good in others, it becomes easier to love them. And the same is true of loving ourselves.

> When we focus on the good in others, it becomes easier to love them. And the same is true of loving ourselves.

SHK 2:290

Wandering Freely

What spark in these writings of Rav Kook resonates with you?

- *Loving others demands extensive work, to expand it to the scope it deserves, to fight against superficiality, shallow impressions, and not fully developed awareness.*

- *We should only feel repulsion for the person's unscrupulous acts, while still valuing and loving their being created in the Image of God.*

- *It is great, illumining work to look at everyone with 'beautiful eyes', with boundless compassion, to emulate 'God's eyes', even for the most iniquitous.*

- *One needs to torture oneself to love human beings … one needs to see their beneficial light through which the radiance of God spreads in the world.*

- *When one really looks at the good side of each and every person, then one falls in love with everyone with a soulful affection. We need to have compassion for others, especially when they disappoint us, to find the positive in them, to amplify their virtues.*

Connecting to our Lives

☑ *What would be different if you looked at people with "beautiful eyes"?*

☑ *Try walking through a mall or shopping area and intentionally see everyone with "beautiful eyes", with "God's eyes". Do you see people differently? How does this make you feel?*

☑ *Look at yourself with "beautiful eyes". Do you see a different self?*

Loving One's Nation

I have lived in the State of Israel for over 40 years and would unequivocally say that loving the Jewish people is absolutely my biggest spiritual challenge. It is an ongoing test, arising anew each day. The diversity of the people, the political ideologies, and the varied lifestyles seem to foster constant bickering and conflict, often resulting in harsh, tactless animosity. Sometimes, for me at least, loving the Jewish People seems to be an impossible aspiration. Living in Israel is like being at a never-ending family reunion of a dysfunctional family. The annoying relatives never go home!

Elie Wiesel was once asked: "What is your favorite place in the world?" He answered: "Jerusalem. When I am not there". Wow! Such an insightful response. It is so much easier to love the *idea* of the Jewish people than to love the actual reality of being with Jews all the time.

For Rav Kook, however, loving the Jewish People was not a challenge but a gift — one which never stopped flowing.

> And there is a person who sings the song of the nation.
> He steps forward from his private soul,
> which he finds narrow...

Yearning to Grow

What is holding me back from loving the Jewish People more?

97

He clings with a sensitive love
to the entirety of the Jewish nation
and sings its song.
He shares in its pains,
is joyful in its hopes,
speaks with exalted and pure thoughts
regarding its past and its future,
and seeks its inner spiritual nature
with love and a wise heart.

SHK 7:112

Rav Kook sang the song of his nation, the Jewish People, with "love and a wise heart".

But this love did not make him blind to the nation's faults:

The great love with which we love our nation
will not cause us to turn a blind eye
to criticizing any of its flaws.

SHK 3:345

Loving a particular nation can have a shadow side; one can love one's nation so much that there is no room for loving other nations. During Rav Kook's lifetime, this kind of excessive love for particular nations led to disastrous xenophobic tendencies, and eventually brought about "the war to end all wars". Living through World War I, Rav Kook was well aware of the dangers of loving one's nation blindly. Hence, he sought to place his love for the Jewish People into the larger context of loving *all* nations.

Loving a particular nation can have a shadow side; one can love one's nation so much that there is no room for loving other nations.

Loving one's nation to the exclusion of others Rav Kook called "small love". He offers blistering criticism of zealous nationality, and cautions against the small-mindedness of loving one's nation too much.

Only upon an enlightened soul,
who loves all creation and all people,
will the love of one's nation rest blessedly.
Small-mindedness,

which causes one to see everything other
than our special nation as ugly and impure,
is one of the most horrible examples of darkness,
which causes blatant destruction
to all beneficial spiritual advancement.

SHK 1:593

According to Rav Kook, the nation of Israel is not the only "chosen" nation. Rather, every nation was chosen — for different purposes and contributions to humankind.

God did a great kindness with the world
by not bequeathing all
the gifts and talents in one place -
not in one person,
and not in one people,
and not in one country.

Orot Yisrael 5:2

Every nation possesses unique "gifts and talents" and should regard themselves as chosen by God. The ultimate goal and purpose of creation is for all of the nations of the world to manifest their unique gifts and talents in harmony with all other nations. Every nation has a unique note to play in the symphony of humankind.

Yet, even while noticing the potential flaws of national love, Rav Kook remained steadfast in his unconditional love for the Jewish People.

Listen to me,
my people.
From my soul I speak to you,
from the soul of my soul,
I must love you with
endless love.

SHK 1:163

According to Rav Kook, the nation of Israel is not the only "chosen" nation. Rather, every nation was chosen — for different purposes and contributions to humankind.

Rav Kook loved the Jewish People with unconditional love. And as with all of his loving, his love for the Jewish People was neither intellectual nor emotional at its core, but rather soulful. It stemmed from his mystical understanding of the union of the individual soul with the soul of the nation. The soul of the individual Jew is inextricably entwined with the soul of the Jewish People. The individual is one piece, one limb, one cell of the whole collective.

> *The individual soul is drawn from the national entity;*
> *the individual soul is derived from the national collective.*
> *If one were to imagine detaching oneself from the People,*
> *it would be as if one were to detach oneself*
> *from the source of one's own life.*

SHK 1:527

Loving the Jewish people was thus, in essence, an extension of self-love.

The soul is not merely our personal animating force, guiding and directing our lives and destinies. The soul is also part of the greater national soul — one point in a pointillist painting. The full painting is the soul of the Jewish people, with each point an individual soul. In this sense, each point has no meaning when detached from the greater picture; it finds its value only in composition with the other points. If we look too close at a single point we can't envision the whole picture. What's more, we come away with a skewed understanding of the single point.

Being part of the soul of the Jewish People means being chosen to be part of the nation's purpose, destiny, and calling. The shared aspiration of the Jewish People unites all Jews together as soulmates, sharing a vision beyond each personal life. The journey toward this common aim inspires and elevates each Jew, as well as the Jewish People as a whole. Rav Kook saw the mission and the dream of the Jewish People as nothing less than bringing about universal oneness:

> *The soul of the Jewish People*
> *strives to heal the entire world.*

Wow! The ultimate vision and responsibility.

> The soul is not merely our personal animating force, guiding and directing our lives and destinies; the soul is also part of the greater national soul — one point in a pointillist painting.

SHK 5:51

Even if vast swaths of the Jewish People are not consciously aware of this mission, and even if they are seemingly oblivious to any shared aspiration, Rav Kook believed in the mystical bonds uniting all Jews into one people. This unity is our collective subconscious. This mystical power is always latent within, and is expressed and actualized during certain moments in history. But even when the Jewish People are neither aware of this mystical bond nor actively striving toward this common goal, Rav Kook still fully loved — with "endless love" and a "wise heart" — the heroic aspiration and sublime dream of a people working together to "heal the entire world".

Rav Kook's love for the Jewish People was unconditional. He openly embraced even those Jews who publicly disparaged the Jewish way of life and ostensibly did not share his vision and dream. He sought to find beauty in their attitudes and actions, seeking to judge them positively and even to advocate for them.

> *The wicked,*
> *who act out of principle,*
> *breaking laws not for their own benefit*
> *but to infuriate others -*
> *their souls are very lofty...*
> *within the core essence of their courage*
> *is a spark of holiness.*

Rav Kook regarded those who "broke the laws of Jewish tradition to infuriate others" as an essential component of the Jewish People. Just as crushed grapes cannot become wine without a fermenting agent, so too the Jewish People needed fermenting agents to shake them out of the status quo and bring them to a higher level. "The wicked" who violated Jewish law were essential catalysts of change. The Jewish People needed them.

Rav Kook writes:

Even if vast swaths of the Jewish People are seemingly oblivious to any shared aspiration, Rav Kook believed in the mystical bonds uniting all Jews into one people. This unity is our collective subconscious.

SHK 1:243

There are many thoughts that seemingly
are not harmonious and contradict one another. . .
but a person should not fear this hysteria of differing ideas,
as these thoughts offer fertile ground for growth
when they collide.

SHK 1:571

Far from being threatened by Jews who espoused a different ideology, Rav Kook grasped in this the potential for "fertile ground
for growth" and the hope for an ultimately more beautiful form of
oneness, enhanced by the differences.

Singing the song of the entire nation requires an expansive soul that
can see beneath superficial impressions and celebrate the process of
journeying together toward the oneness of the world.

Singing the song of the entire
nation requires an expansive
soul that can see beneath
superficial impressions and
celebrate the process of
journeying together toward
the oneness of the world.

Wandering Freely

What spark in these writings of Rav Kook resonates with you?

- *The great love with which we love our nation will not cause us to turn a blind eye to criticizing any of its flaws.*

- *Small-mindedness, which causes one to see everything other than our special nation as ugly and impure, is one of the most horrible examples of darkness, which causes blatant destruction to all beneficial spiritual advancement.*

- *God did a great kindness with the world by not bequeathing all the gifts and talents in one place — not in one person and not in one people, and not in one country.*

- *If one were to imagine detaching oneself from the People, it would be as if one were to detach oneself from the source of one's own life.*

- *The soul of the Jewish People strives to heal the entire world.*

- *The wicked, who act out of principle, breaking laws not for their own benefit but to infuriate others — their souls are very lofty … within the core essence of their courage is a spark of holiness.*

Connecting to our Lives

☑ *What aspect of the Jewish People disappoints you?*

☑ *What aspect of the Jewish People inspires you?*

☑ *What group of Jewish people is the most difficult for you to love? Can you find some redeeming quality of their behavior? Imagine for a moment that you were part of that group — what argument could you make in their defense?*

☑ *Purchase a book about the Jewish People or the State of Israel.*

☑ *How connected are you to the Jewish People? What would be different about your life if you were more connected? What is holding you back?*

Loving and Politics

Political animosity is nothing new. Over a century ago, Rav Kook bemoaned the lack of love and oneness in the political domain.

Yearning to Grow

What small step could I take to see the worth and sliver of truth of the other side?

Three forces struggle today in the Jewish People —
the holy, national, and the humanistic.
It would be tragic if these 3 camps that need to help each
other and unite would entrench themselves in extremism.
They must ultimately work together for
there to be hope for the future.
The separating of these drives results from their focus-
ing on the shortcomings of the other 2 forces and
not seeing the flaws in their own group...
The 3 camps are known as:
The Orthodox, who zealously and bitterly defend the Torah,
mitzvot, and all that is holy in Israel.
The new Nationalists, who fight for statehood.
The Liberals [who speak for universal issues].
It is obvious that in a healthy situation there
is a need for all 3 of these forces.

We must continually aspire for this state that the 3 forces
harmoniously and beneficially function together
none of them taking up too much or too little space,
clinging to each other with sublime love —
the holy, the national, and the universal —
each recognizing the important role of the other.

SHK 3:1

In the political world, it is not pragmatic — and perhaps even scary — to acknowledge the credibility of the other side.

In the political world, it is not pragmatic — and perhaps even scary — to acknowledge the credibility of the other side. Rather than cooperate with the other side, we aim to defeat them. We want our side to triumph, and the more decisive the victory, the better. We campaign endlessly to promote our views and to diminish the worth of the other side. We seek out their weakest points, and then, like sharks sensing blood in the water, we strive to obliterate them. The last thing we want to do is grant their viewpoints any legitimacy. Political campaigns are often remarkable in their aggression, their bashing, and their ruthless antagonism.

This hostility builds upon itself. The louder the volume, the more our adrenaline flows, and we feel the thrill of our convictions and the rightfulness of our positions. We applaud those leaders who speak passionately against our opponents.

Personally, I experienced this approach during my years of learning in an Israeli yeshiva. We had a sense that we held the truth. All of the truth. This was an incredibly blissful feeling; it exempted us from ever having to listen to the other side! Simply by virtue of their disagreeing with us we knew they were wrong, their positions untenable. Life was simple and clear: We were right; they were wrong. We saw no merit in any of their viewpoints. Our rightness occasionally brought us to spiritual ecstasy.

This approach epitomizes the antithesis of Rav Kook's goal of bringing oneness into the political realm.

The separating of these drives
results from their focusing
on the shortcomings of the other 2 forces
and not seeing the flaws in their own group.

For Rav Kook, there was no exclusive right or absolute wrong. It was not by chance that numerous viewpoints existed. He saw in each ideology a sliver of the truth. Political wellness depends on the harmony of its parts.

Acknowledging the worth of the other side was not a tactical — or even a strategic — approach for Rav Kook. Nor was he just trying to be nice or to lower the volume of the debate.

These are the three forces that fundamentally com-
pose every individual and collective.

Each human being and each collective lacks some of the wisdom of the other sides. If one side were rendered completely unnecessary, then there would be no potential of including it. Full oneness would never be achieved.

But Rav Kook does not stop with the political feasibility and effectiveness of working together. The aspiration of the different sides functioning together in harmony is only the beginning. He pushes us one step further. We need to: "cling to each other with sublime love."

As we have seen many times, there is no oneness without love, there is no functioning "harmoniously and beneficially together" without love.

Rav Kook envisioned sublime love — radiant and holy — even in the political realm.

Living in Israel, I have found love to be pretty hard to actualize in the political arena. Just a few days after the last election in Israel, during which the ultra-orthodox parties acquired much greater power, there was a knock on my door. It was evening and I anticipated someone

Political wellness depends on the harmony of its parts.

asking for tzedakah (charity). When I opened the door there stood a young man in full black ultra-orthodox garb with a pleasant smile on his face. He said that he was raising money to buy Shabbat food for needy families in his community. In truth, even before he opened his mouth, I was already irritated. As a staunch Zionist, with my children having spent many years as soldiers and officers in the Israeli Army, I felt that it was the height of chutzpah for an anti-Zionist organization to ask for money for anti-Zionist families, from a Zionist household.

We engaged in some small talk but I couldn't hold back. "What do you think of the new government?" I asked. "Do you think we're moving in a good direction?"

I was relieved when he diplomatically skirted the question. "I just want what's good for everyone," he said.

But then he added that at least the new government wouldn't ruin everything like the last government had done, and my blood began to boil. My voice remained calm as I drilled him with questions and clamored about all the flaws of the new government and its religious orientation.

Eventually, I gave him a moderately generous contribution and wished him the best.

Afterwards, I was really upset with myself. Infuriated! How could I allow myself to be so provoked? What brought me to such resentment and anger — to almost exploding at the fellow? Was my study of Rav Kook's wisdom and his focus on loving completely meaningless?

About an hour later I reflected a bit more on the incident. While my behavior was egregiously disappointing, I was probably a little gentler, a little softer, and a little more measured than I would have been a few years back, before I began to delve into Rav Kook's wisdom. Perhaps the learning was not pointless after all! Perhaps it had enabled me to take a small step. I chuckled as I thought that I was actually looking forward to the next time the young man knocked on my door to see if I could take another small step toward loving someone who espoused beliefs so antithetical to my own.

Was his sliver of truth the "fertile ground" I needed for my own personal growth?

Wandering Freely

What spark in these writings of Rav Kook resonates with you?

- *It would be tragic if these 3 camps — that need to help each other and unite — would entrench themselves in extremism.*

- *The separating of these drives results from their focusing on the shortcomings of the other 2 forces and not seeing the flaws in their own group .*

- *We must continually aspire for this state — that the 3 forces harmoniously and beneficially function together — none of them taking up too much or too little space, clinging to each other with sublime love.*

Was this stranger's sliver of truth the "fertile ground" I needed for my own personal growth?

Connecting to our Lives

☑ *Notice when you get triggered in a political conversation. What buttons of yours were pressed?*

☑ *What sliver of truth can you find in opposing political groups?*

☑ *What flaws do you see in the political views that you espouse?*

☑ *Seek out someone who is on the opposite end of the political spectrum. Let go of the debating, persuading, and negating. Try to listen. Find the element of truth in their viewpoint.*

☑ *Try to love the other person even while disagreeing with their political opinion.*

LOVING ONESELF

A person must believe in one's life.

Loving Myself

T he first obligation in loving all people is for us to love ourselves. Tragically, this seems to be a very hard thing to do.

For three years I worked as an educational consultant for Hillel International, visiting countless universities from coast to coast. "How much do you love yourselves?" I often asked college students. "On a scale from 1 to 10, what number would you give yourself?" The answers were usually between 4 and 6. In a regular class, that's a failing grade.

Most people I know, regardless of age, find it much easier to criticize than to praise themselves. And, even though criticizing ourselves can push us toward greater achievement, more often than not it is unhelpful, and sometimes downright exhausting, leaving us empty and deflated.

Rav Kook writes,

> *Love should be with a full heart — for all people.*

"For all people" includes — even and especially — ourselves.

We set noble expectations for ourselves, often demanding excellence, even perfection. We continually beat ourselves up when we fall short.

Yearning to Grow

What advice would I give to myself to become more comfortable talking about my best qualities?

SHK 1:807

113

Countless times I've heard from friends and students: "It's easier for me to believe in someone else than to believe in myself. I am always letting myself down. I know better than anyone else how much I mess up. Not a day goes by that I do not screw up something. How can I love someone who never fulfills their potential and continually disappoints me?"

Often the expectations and standards we set for ourselves are dictated by others — our family, community, and society. Success is measured relative to *being better* than others. A friend once told me that he holds himself to a "very high" standard. I responded that "very high" is a comparative measure; something can only be "very high" in contrast to something else. Who is he comparing himself to? Comparing ourselves to others will inevitably lead to low self-esteem and self-loathing. There will always be someone achieving more.

I once asked a group of students, "What would happen to you if your jealousy of others just miraculously vanished? Poof! It's gone. Disappeared forever."

After a few moments of stunned silence, one student said, "I would be more present and content. I would taste true peace and freedom." The group laughed when someone commented, "Well, that sure would free up a lot of time."

Jealousy has nothing to do with the other person. Jealousy occurs when we *do not accept who we are.* Jealousy occurs when we forget the root of our soul. It is this forgetfulness of our own worth that leads to jealousy. And when we are jealous of others, it is virtually impossible to be happy for them. We can only be happy for others if we accept and love ourselves.

We need to hold ourselves, not to a "very high standard," but to "our standard" — the standard that is appropriate for our current level of achievement and growth. Each of us has a different standard. And

> Jealousy has nothing to do with the other person. Jealousy occurs when we do not accept who we are.

each of us can take small steps to reach that standard. Rav Kook writes,

Every person has a moral obligation to advance themselves.

SHK 2:339

We need to advance ourselves and hold ourselves accountable, but only to the potential that is fitting for our personal soul root, our own personal history and condition.

Loving others begins with loving ourselves. Love for ourselves, just like the love for others, should not be conditional. How many of us love ourselves more when we are having a successful day? When we are being productive and achieving a lot?

But no one has only successful days. Loving ourselves should not be a function of our successes, or our actions and behavior. It cannot be anchored in how we are doing. If our opinion of ourselves is based on our performance, then our self-love will always be conditional. Throughout our lives we will experience endless successes and failures, highlights and low points, achievements and disappointments. If loving ourselves is based on how we are doing, then we are setting ourselves up for life on an emotional roller coaster.

Rav Kook writes:

A person must believe in one's life.

Before we see the light of God in other people, we need to see it in ourselves. The same students and friends who lament that it is so hard to love and support themselves will often comment that they do not see anything special or extraordinary about themselves. When I ask them to write about their shortcomings, they do not hesitate to fill page after page. But when I ask them to write about their praiseworthy qualities and acts, they are often stumped. Many of them have trouble even picking up the pen. After a few moments they say, "It's hard for me to think of any. I am just an ordinary person."

> Love for ourselves, just like the love for others, should not be conditional. If loving ourselves is based on how we are doing, then we are setting ourselves up for life on an emotional roller coaster.

SHK 1:231

But there are no "ordinary" people! Everyone is uniquely special, chosen, and brought into this world by God to play an irreplaceable role. Rav Kook writes that there are no duplicate souls (SHK 2:241). We need to unconditionally believe that God has chosen us, despite — and even with — all of our shortcomings and flaws.

Nevertheless, there seems to be an inner reluctance to loving ourselves. Doesn't it seem a bit self-centered, egotistical, or even arrogant to focus on loving ourselves? Aren't we encouraged to be giving people, seeking what is best for others, and to be humble regarding our own qualities?

Rav Kook writes,

> *One should be more wary of low self-esteem than of arrogance.*

Arrogance, while clearly not praiseworthy, is easier to fix than low self-esteem. Sometime, somewhere, someone is going to make me aware of being arrogant. And if I don't learn from the first person who points it out, then hopefully I will learn it from the second or third person who admonishes me. Hopefully, I will learn how to tone down and reappraise how I view myself.

But low self-esteem is much harder to correct than arrogance. If someone points it out to me and encourages me to have more regard for myself, to be proud of myself, it's just so easy to shrug off their advice. It's so easy not to take their words seriously. I can just say to myself: "They don't really know me".

Rav Kook writes,

> *Every individual needs to find oneself in one's self,*
> *and afterward one finds oneself*
> *in one's surroundings, community, and people.*

It is hard work to reframe how we look at ourselves, to love ourselves unconditionally. It is hard work to believe in ourselves and accept

---

But there are no "ordinary" people! Everyone is uniquely special, chosen, and brought into this world by God to play an irreplaceable role.

SHK 1:894

SHK 8:46

that we each possess a unique root of our soul.

But this lack of love for ourselves is a catastrophe of the greatest proportions. If we do not firmly and unconditionally believe that we are each chosen by God, then it is unlikely that we will see this in others. *Loving other people begins with loving ourselves!*

For Rav Kook, loving ourselves stems from believing that we each have a unique soul root, and therefore a unique calling and purpose in life. The world needs me.

Rav Kook wrote about himself,

> It is not for no reason that God
> implanted within me the insatiable desire for all that is hidden,
> for all that is mystical and otherworldly.
> It is not for no reason that God
> brought me to Eretz Yisrael.
> It is not for no reason that God
> created within me a pure and courageous spirit.

Implicit in Rav Kook's refrain of "It is not for no reason" was his belief in the holiness and importance of his path. God had a plan for him. His life circumstances and innate abilities were not random or meaningless. There was *a reason* for each of his qualities. His life and abilities reflected God's trust in him to bring about whatever healing he could provide for this beautiful and broken world. God spoke to him through the voice of his soul, sending him signs, guiding him, and urging him forward.

Rav Kook looked into himself and saw a divine mystery. He saw the soul as a divine gift of infinite layers that needed to be continually unwrapped. Each time he unwrapped this gift and revealed an inner layer, he uncovered a deeper sense of clarity into his true gifts and nature, enabling him to better shine his light into this world. There were endless layers to be unwrapped.

If we do not firmly and unconditionally believe that we are each chosen by God, then it is unlikely that we will see this in others. Loving other people begins with loving ourselves!

SHK 3:259

This is the secret of loving ourselves that Rav Kook has shown us: the more we unwrap and reveal deeper truths of ourselves, the more we discover our future beckoning to us. There is always more to love.

This unknown and undisclosed future ultimately gives purpose and meaning to our lives. The future sanctifies our present. In a profound moment of counterintuitive wisdom, Rav Kook teaches us that we derive our self-worth not from our past achievements, but from our future promise! The love we have for ourselves grows out of our unshakable belief that God sees us as having something precious and unique to offer the world.

Self-love is a love of what we are called to become.

How do we unwrap this gift of our unique soul? How do we gain clarity into our future direction?

Rav Kook writes,

> *I need to talk a lot about myself.*
> *My essential self must become utterly clear to me.*
> *Through understanding myself*
> *I will come to understand everything —*
> *the world and life —*
> *until I will come to understand*
> *the source of all life.*

"I need to talk a lot about myself" — not a little but "a lot." Why? So that "my essential self becomes utterly clear to me."

This goal of self-knowledge for Rav Kook was not self-serving. His goal was not only to understand himself but also to understand "the world and life," and ultimately to gain clarity into "the source of all life." Rav Kook sought to understand his role in the larger picture of creation.

Our unknown and undisclosed future ultimately gives purpose and meaning to our lives. The future sanctifies our present.

SHK 7:189

There is a paradox here: We cannot discover self-love through focusing on ourselves. Loving ourselves stems from our belief that we are needed in the world. Loving ourselves emerges from the awareness of our responsibility — and great privilege — to contribute to the bigger picture. Only through gaining clarity into the world, life, and the source of all life, can we fully begin to understand ourselves. Through this understanding of self comes the unconditional love and awareness of our true gifts. Every person needs to believe "It is not for no reason that I exist. I have a future path. I need to believe in myself and, especially, to believe in what I can become."

Rav Kook adds that it is never easy to unwrap the gift of one's soul. It requires constant focus, intentionality, and work.

> *As one grows spiritually,*
> *one's mysterious soul becomes*
> *more and more concealed from one's own self-awareness,*
> *and one needs to invest more in searching for oneself.*
> *One needs to dedicate more time in aloneness.*

I never arrive at the innermost truth of my soul. Despite unwrapping layer after layer, like a Russian matryoshka doll, there is always another layer to be revealed. According to Rav Kook, I am on a never-ending path of discovery of who I am and who I can become. I am always living in a state of becoming, a work-in-progress. I can always become a kinder, more loving, more giving, better version of what I am right now. The soul has infinite layers.

Just as I need to invest effort in loving myself for my unique soul, so too, I need to work to love my body — for it too is uniquely mine. Tragically though, these days it seems that one of the hardest things for most people to accept, appreciate, and love is their own bodies.

I cannot begin to count how many times I have heard family members, friends, colleagues, and students complain about their bodies. They

> We cannot discover self-love through focusing on ourselves. Loving ourselves stems from our belief that we are needed in the world.
>
> SHK 8:149

wish they were taller; they wish they were thinner. They wish that their noses were a bit smaller; they wish their hair was a different texture or color. I know people who have groaned for decades about the five or ten extra pounds they've been trying to lose.

And on the other hand, how many times have I heard someone say: "Oh, *that* person has a great body".

The truth is — we all have perfect bodies. That is to say, we all have the appropriate bodies for our souls. We all have been gifted the optimal bodies to manifest the work of our souls. It is a perfect match.

Our souls and our bodies are not two separate disconnected entities. We have unique faces, bodies, and voices precisely because we have unique souls. I have exactly the face I am supposed to have. I have exactly the face I need to have to fulfill my role in this world. It is the perfect expression of my soul. The body matches the soul; for our souls to best actualize themselves in this world, we were given precisely the body necessary to fulfill our calling. The soul can't do anything without the body.

My physical nature is not by chance; it is not a mistake. It was not just a random happening that I am this height, with this face, and with this color hair. My body was expertly designed by the Maker of my soul; it is the clothing for my soul. Rav Kook refers to God as an architect of physicality. There is a reason I am not taller, more coordinated, and do not have a better singing voice.

Writes Rav Kook:

> We see the organic nature
> of the physical and spiritual reality.
> We can clearly perceive that everything operates together
> and is always working together on everything.

We all have been gifted the optimal bodies to manifest the work of our souls. It is a perfect match!

SHK 5:59

I am composed of both a spiritual and physical reality. The physical is the vehicle through which the spiritual is revealed. We have mysterious souls and perfect bodies. There is a lot about ourselves worthy of love.

Wandering Freely

What spark in these writings of Rav Kook resonates with you?

- *Love should be with a full-heart — for all people.*

- *Every person has a moral obligation to advance themselves. A person must believe in one's life.*

- *One should be more wary of low self-esteem than of arrogance.*

- *Every individual needs to find oneself in one's self, and afterward one finds oneself in one's surroundings, community, and people.*

- *It is not for no reason that God . . .*

- *I need to talk a lot about myself. My essential self must become utterly clear to me. Through understanding myself I will come to understand everything — the world and life — until I will come to understand the source of all life.*

- *As one grows spiritually, one's mysterious soul becomes more and more concealed from one's own self-awareness, and one needs to invest more in searching for oneself. One needs to dedicate more time in aloneness*

- *We see the organic nature of the physical and spiritual reality. For sure, we can perceive that everything operates together and is always working together on everything*

Connecting to our Lives

- ☑ *On a scale of 1-10: How much do you love yourself?*

- ☑ *How would your life be different if you magically jumped up a number or two?*

- ☑ *What are your most praiseworthy virtues? List at least 5.*

- ☑ *Finish this sentence: "It is not for no reason that God made me … and gave me …*

- ☑ *Ask three of your friends what they most like and appreciate about you.*

- ☑ *What do you need to do to love your body more?*

Loving Myself
Is Hard Work

E ven if we believe that we have been bequeathed a unique soul root and that we have an essential role to play in the future unfolding of the world, what about all of our mess-ups? What about those traits of ours that we find frustrating and intolerable? What about those things we do that we know are not okay? Shouldn't those diminish our love for ourselves?

Rav Kook urges us to appreciate our whole selves. Both our strengths and our weaknesses are necessary and God-given.

> *When one becomes aware of one's essence,*
> *then one realizes that everything one needs*
> *to fulfill one's purpose in life*
> *has been beneficially bequeathed to him (or her)*
> *through the compassion of the Creator.*
> *Both one's positive and negative attributes*
> *are needed and are gifts from above.*

"Both one's positive and negative attributes are needed and are gifts from above" — wow! Are my shortcomings, limitations, and flaws also God-given? Are they also blessings? Apparently.

Yearning to Grow

For what behavior of mine do I need to become more forgiving?

Olat HaRa'aya

123

Rav Kook writes that I need to forgive myself for my shortcomings, forget my mess-ups, and even celebrate my mistakes!

But loving myself with a full heart is so difficult. Even if I can begin to accept that my "positive and negative attributes are needed and are gifts from above," nevertheless, I still have to deal with all of my bad decisions, errors in judgment, and endless bungling. I have so many regrets. There are so many moments in my life that I wish I could do over; things I did and even more — things I should have done. So many words I wish I could take back. So many words that others really needed to hear but never made it out of my mouth. I have let many people down in my life. Not to mention the countless times I have let myself down. There is not enough time in the day for me to reflect on all the things in my past that I would like to change.

I can accept that somewhere in God's eternal plan it is not realistic for me to be gifted in everything. I can accept God giving me negative attributes, troublesome inclinations like impulsivity and stubbornness. I can accept that it was destined for me to have a terrible singing voice. But how does that in any way excuse my forgetting my wife's birthday, losing my temper with my children, or being afraid to leave my job and start something new, which I know I should have done. How can I let all that go? These were my decisions alone, made of my own free will, not destined from above.

Rav Kook would tell me that I'm going about it all wrong. I have to let go of this old script of regret, shame, and self-reproach. They are not worthy to guide me. Life is a long journey and I cannot move ahead on my path while still carrying the heavy baggage of my past.

First, Rav Kook would tell me that I need to reframe how I look at myself. I need to forgive myself for my shortcomings and endless mess-ups.

> Life is a long journey and I cannot move ahead on my path while still carrying the heavy baggage of my past.

> *The first step*
> *to alleviate the anguish*
> *of disappointing behavior*
> *is to forgive oneself,*
> *and then afterward*
> *to forgive others.*

SHK 2:150

I have asked many students, "What would happen if, on the self-forgiveness scale of 1 to 10, you miraculously became a 9.5?" The most common responses were, "I wouldn't be second-guessing myself all the time. I would become more compassionate. I would become a better friend, a better partner." Our mess-ups become exaggerated when we cannot let go of them: when they continue to reverberate and take up emotional bandwidth. They're unbearably heavy weights to carry around, impeding our love for ourselves and others.

Rav Kook instructs us not to wallow in the past, not to continually chew on all the things we have done wrong. We will never live a perfect day, nor even a perfect hour.

What would happen if, on the self-forgiveness scale of 1 to 10, you miraculously became a 9.5?

Second, even more than to forgive, Rav Kook writes, we should try to *forget* our flawed behavior!

> *It is good to forget one's sins,*
> *when one does this with integrity*
> *to improve the world*
> *and serve God with joy.*

SHK 6:258

> *One should not dwell on past failings,*
> *as any dwelling on fixing past flaws*
> *will prevent one from growing*
> *and place many obstacles*
> *on the path of change.*

Orot HaTeshuvah 13:9

Rav Kook would tell me that I should always be looking ahead. It's all about my next steps. The questions I need to dwell on are:

* How can I best move forward?

* How can I become a better version of myself — tomorrow, next week, and for the rest of my life?

This does not mean that we should be easy on ourselves. This does not mean that we should not try to learn from our mistakes. We need to reflect, acknowledge, and own everything we have done. We focus on our past as it helps us learn about ourselves and prevents us from repeating the same mistakes. We delve into all the causes and nuances of what we did, understand it deeply, and hopefully discover what led us to mess up.

But there is a grave danger inherent in this process. When we dwell on our past shortcomings, we run the risk of paralyzing ourselves. Rav Kook would tell us that we should minimize the analyzing and reanalyzing of our past shortcomings; if we plunge into the mud of our lives, we will only emerge muddy. We need to treat ourselves with love and kindness. We need to move on. We need to let it go. We need to continually treat ourselves with generous mercy. With "beautiful eyes". Otherwise, we will never move ahead.

How can we move toward loving ourselves when we are continually reminding ourselves how we failed to live up to our expectations? How can we move toward loving ourselves when we are continually berating ourselves?

We need to forgive. We need to forget.

Third and most important, not only do we need to forgive and forget our shortcomings, but we should also celebrate them!

Rav Kook writes,

> How can we move toward loving ourselves when we are continually reminding ourselves how we failed to live up to our expectations?

I will not let my failings bring me down,
as I know that all of them are necessary,
and will serve as springboards for my growth.

SHK 6:9

Failing as necessary? Springboards for growth?

We are always messing up. We need to make mistakes; they are the "springboards for growth." Instead of judging ourselves harshly for our mistakes, we need to recognize that we need them. They are opportunities for growth.

Growth is never a simple, straightforward, or smooth process. When all is going well, there is little or no impetus for change. When things are going well, we want to preserve the status quo. While this may be gratifying, it is also a trap. The status quo will never make us better; the status quo never impels us to grow.

Mess-ups shake us up; mess-ups undo our complacency. The crises unbalance us, "destuckify" us. The crises in our lives provide opportunities for change and growth. I never intentionally blunder, but apparently deep within my bungling are the seeds for the next stage of my life. Apparently, I needed to make those mistakes to rethink my actions and ultimately get to where I need to be.

> We are always messing up. We need to make mistakes; they are the "springboards for growth."

Sometimes the blessings in life are clear and self-evident — blessings in broad daylight. Sometimes, blessings come in the blackness of night. They are cloaked in darkness and seem impenetrable. But like the night, they can give birth to a new day. The poet Mary Oliver writes in "The Uses of Sorrow," "Someone I loved once gave me a box full of darkness. It took me years to understand that this, too, was a gift."

Rav Kook writes:

There is a spark of light and holiness in every failing.
The wise ones seek it out and grow from it.

SHK 2:350

127

"Seek it out and grow from it". Even our mess-ups have "a spark of light and holiness".

We have to be careful here. Telling others that their failings are necessary and they can grow from it can be glib, callous, and self-serving. Telling others that they need to learn from their mistakes can be sanctimonious and self-righteous. Rav Kook was writing to himself, in the privacy and sanctity of his own soul. He was admonishing himself.

Recently two of our kids had a falling out. One of them blurted out a comment about the other's spouse that crossed a line and caused a rift in their relationship. Their first attempt to talk it out and make peace ended disastrously. They were both quite bummed out. They turned to me for advice and, guided by Rav Kook's wisdom, I suggested they reframe what they initially considered to be a mess-up and look at it as an invitation to discover a deeper level of their relationship. It was an unplanned and unexpected opportunity for growth. And that's exactly how it eventually played out. Their relationship grew from it.

"The wise ones seek it out and grow from it".

Even our mess-ups have
"a spark of light and holiness".

Wandering Freely

What spark in these writings of Rav Kook resonates with you?

🌀 *When one becomes aware of one's essence, then one realizes that everything one needs to fulfill one's purpose in life has been beneficially bequeathed to him or her through the compassion of the Creator. Both one's positive and negative attributes are needed and are gifts from above.*

🌀 *The first step to alleviate the anguish of disappointing behavior is to forgive oneself, and then afterward to forgive others.*

🌀 *It is good to forget one's sins, when one does this with integrity to improve the world and serve God with joy. One should not dwell on past failings, as any dwelling on fixing past flaws will prevent one from growing and place many obstacles on the path of change.*

🌀 *I will not let my failings bring me down, as I know that all of them are necessary, and will serve as springboards for my growth.*

🌀 *There is a spark of light and holiness in every failing. The wise ones seek it out and grow from it.*

Connecting to our Lives

☑ *Do you chew on your mistakes and disappointments? Do they take up a lot of your emotional bandwidth?*

☑ *What strategy could you adopt to let them go?*

☑ *Write yourself a letter. Begin with: "I forgive you for (at least 3 actions)..."*

☑ *What mess-ups of yours proved ultimately to be springboards for growth? List at least 3.*

Loving & Forgiving

Yearning to Grow

What relationship of mine could be
healed through forgiveness?

Love is the vehicle for bringing people together. Love brings oneness into the world.

But what happens when relationships break down? What happens when connections unravel? When things go awry? What happens when oneness is lost? How can we restore oneness?

Forgiveness — that's what needs to happen. We need to ask for forgiveness. And we need to offer forgiveness.

Forgiveness is the medicine necessary to heal brokenness. In the daily standing prayer (*Amidah*) we refer to God as the one who "forgives a lot" (*Marbeh l'sloah*). God doesn't just forgive. God forgives "a lot". Forgiveness on steroids.

Forgiveness is the first cousin of love. Forgiveness emerges from our soul; forgiveness emerges when we tap into our higher selves. Forgiveness emerges from the same source as our seeking oneness.

Rav Kook writes:

> *Holy forgiveness emerges from the Source of kindness,*
> *From the expansive endless ultimate greatness.*

SHK 5:193

131

When we do not — or cannot — forgive, the breakdown in relationship gnaws at us. It doesn't just go away, no matter how much we try to ignore or repress it. The passing of time does not heal the brokenness. The relationship does not magically heal itself. Our wallowing in its collapse only adds to the toxic stones gathering around our heart. The issues need to be directly owned, acknowledged, and addressed. And it is so hard.

For some reason, it seems harder to say "I am sorry" than to say "I love you".

Saying "I love you" can be thrilling, can be hopeful — even daring. It is a step forward in the relationship. The vulnerability of loving brings with it a sense of living on the edge, of being fully alive. It is a step toward an unknown future, moving a relationship to a new and deeper level.

Even the love aligned with Rav Kook's sense of love — not as an emotion but as a deep wisdom — can make a person feel more in harmony with the depth of their soul.

But forgiveness is a different kind of oneness; it brings with it a different type of sensation. Saying "I'm sorry", "I regret what I did", "I'm embarrassed and a bit ashamed of my behavior, please forgive me", carries none of the enchantment of saying "I love you". Forgiveness can be a taste of oneness that is difficult to swallow.

Years ago, when my son Amichai was 13 or 14 years old, I committed one of the stupidest acts of my parenting career. It was late Friday afternoon, we needed to get to a friends' house to light Shabbat candles and were running late. It was a 25-minute walk, and the sun was already setting. We were cutting it very close. I urged the children to grab their things so we could get a move on. Amichai was upstairs. He came down wearing his weekday sneakers. I told him to go upstairs and put on his Shabbat shoes. "You know you

> For some reason, it seems harder to say "I am sorry" than to say "I love you".

can't wear sneakers on Shabbat".

Amichai said that his sneakers were more comfortable. It was a long walk and he wanted to wear them.

I wouldn't budge. Feeling the clock moving and the sun going down, I raised my voice and told him to go change into his Shabbat shoes.

Then, Amichai went into slow-motion. He deliberately and unhurriedly took it step by step, barely moving. Painstakingly slow. I started to lose it. I was going through a ton of pressure at work and had had a very bad week. My fuse was precariously short. I yelled at him to move faster. He started to descend, now wearing his Shabbat shoes, moving in the tiniest imperceptible steps.

I unraveled. I screamed for him to come down. In a moment, I saw a flash of panic on his face. He scampered down the steps and ran out the front door, running away toward the neighborhood park.

Now I was totally adrift. Furious with myself for losing my temper over something as silly as Shabbat shoes, I told Sandra to take the rest of the kids and start walking. I would go look for Amichai.

He was at the edge of the park. I approached. He took a step backwards. Step toward; step away. I had no idea what to do. Finally, I just sat down on a bench in the park. Amichai gradually came over and sat on the far end of the bench. We sat in silence.

In my mind, I was replaying the scenario and was utterly befuddled as to what to do next.

I was clearly wrong. No question about it. No doubt. He's just a kid who wanted to wear comfortable shoes. I was the adult in the room and had behaved ridiculously. I was a terrible role model.

But what should I do now? Should I apologize? I didn't know if I should or not. In my long relationship with my father, he had never apologized to me over anything. His father, my grandfather, had never apologized to him. And my great-grandfather, who I had known pretty well, was absolutely not the "I'm sorry" kind of guy. In my family, we had a tradition spanning generations of fathers not apologizing to their sons. Sandra, my wife, has no problem saying, "I'm sorry". But maybe it was different for men? For fathers? I didn't know. Someone had forgotten to give me that memo. Would it completely upset the rules of fathering if I apologized? Maybe we were supposed to be strong invincible role models. Would apologizing somehow upset the cosmic balance of the world? What if I asked for forgiveness and he threw it back in my face?

I had no idea what to do.

We sat in silence and then I said to myself: "What the heck. I was wrong. And if I upset the order of the universe, so be it. He's a good kid and deserves more".

"Amichai, I'm sorry." I said. "It was stupid of me to make you change your shoes. I'm sorry that I yelled at you. I'm sorry if I scared you. I feel like a failure of a father".

More silence.

Then Amichai said one of the most beautiful things I have ever heard from our children. He said: "Abba, when my friends and I get together, they all complain about their fathers. I say that when I grow up I want to be just like you".

Apologizing. Forgiveness. Healing the brokenness; renewing the oneness.

Rav Kook writes that:

> *The appearance of the light of kindness and forgiveness*
> *is a sign of spiritual growth;*
> *of feeling more deeply the need for oneness.*

Would it completely upset the rules of fathering if I apologized? Would it lessen my standing as a role model?

SHK 1:708

He writes of the spiritual celebration of Yom Kippur, when we bask the whole day in the air of forgiveness.

> *In the all-embracing state of forgiveness*
> *present on Yom Kippur*
> *there is a holy radiance.*

SHK 5:193

It is the radiance of oneness; the radiance of repairing brokenness. The radiance of forgiveness and love.

The anti-hero of Yom Kippur is Jonah the prophet. Jonah runs away from God. Not because he does not believe in God, but because he rejects God's predilection for forgiving. Jonah thinks that God forgives too easily. God knew that Jonah would run away. God chose Jonah precisely *because* he would run away. God wanted to teach him the spiritual truth and necessity of forgiveness. Jonah wanted to live in a world of strict and clear justice. God chose Jonah precisely to teach him the beauty and value of forgiveness.

It's not clear if Jonah ever learned this lesson from God.

I needed to learn it from a young boy.

God chose Jonah precisely to teach him the beauty and value of forgiveness.

Wandering Freely

What spark in these writings of Rav Kook resonates with you?

 The appearance of the light of kindness and forgiveness is a sign of spiritual growth; of feeling more deeply the need for oneness.

 In the all-embracing state of forgiveness present on Yom Kippur there is a holy radiance.

Connecting to our Lives

☑ *Who was the last person for whom you found the inner strength and love to forgive? How did you feel afterward?*

☑ *Who do you need to forgive now? Can you pick up the phone or write a letter to that person?*

☑ *What would be different in your life if you became a person who forgives "a lot"?*

OBSTACLES TO LOVING

Too much love
cannot sustain a relationship
for a long period of time.

We restore love for this world through prayer.

Loving Others
Too Much

Is it possible to love too much?

According to Rav Kook, we need to continually strive to expand our love, to deepen our love, to work very hard not to let our love become small or limited. We need to love ourselves and stretch ourselves to expand the circles of our love to more and more people. This is how we reflect God's endless love for all of creation.

So, if this is the unceasing aspiration of our lives, should there be any limit to our loving? Rav Kook writes,

> *Too much love*
> *cannot sustain a relationship*
> *for a long period of time.*

Wow! Doesn't this sentence contradict everything we have said till now?!

The goal of love is not only love. The goal of loving is not only loving.

The goal of love and loving — both the noun and the verb — is to engender and *sustain* loving relationships.

Yearning to Grow

Is there any relationship in my life which could benefit from clearer boundaries?

SHK 1:444

For our relationships to stand the test of time, we need to periodically place boundaries on our giving and our kindness. Sometimes we need to restrict our loving. In Kabbalistic terms, we need to express "*din*" ("judgment") and limit the explicit display of our loving. This could be evident in serious disagreements with people we love very much, or even in tiny moments of friction with people we barely know, like someone taking a parking place or butting in ahead of us at the grocery store.

In one of his most shocking observations, Rav Kook writes that King Saul was on a higher level than the future King David, as Saul had mercy and compassion even on Amalek, the epitome of evil. King Saul showed love even for his mortal enemy. Then Rav Kook adds, "But this quality of kindness can only prepare kingship. It cannot sustain it for a long period of time".

To sustain a relationship over time, according to Rav Kook, we cannot behave only with love and kindness. Sometimes we need to look out more for our own well-being. Sometimes we need to confront and reprove the other person. Sometimes we need to judge the other person for the sake of the relationship.

The question is, how do we express *din* in our love? What is our tone of voice? Are we angry? Are we resentful? Is there a trace of self-righteousness? When we judge another person, when we say things that may be difficult for him or her to hear and acknowledge, what energy are we working off?

Can I breathe love — even into my withholding of love?

Can I not abandon my loving even while expressing strong judgment?

Can I withhold love — lovingly?

At first glance, this would seem to be an impossible task. Precisely those issues that bring me to confront other people may eclipse

> For our relationships to stand the test of time, we need to periodically place boundaries on our giving and our kindness. Sometimes we need to restrict our loving.
>
> SHK 1:444

my love for them at that moment. For me personally, potentially stressful conversations have always been difficult. As a middle child, I was the peacemaker and avoided conflict. On the other hand, as an adult, I often looked at these potentially hostile conversations as battles that I needed to win, and the tone of my voice often morphed into self-righteousness, becoming aggressive and combative. My goal was not to lose face, not to appear weak, and to make my points successfully and convincingly. During these interactions, love was nowhere to be found.

Rav Kook offers us a very different approach.

> *The limiting of love*
> *breathes with hidden love.*
> *When love must limit itself,*
> *it limits its love — with love.*

The question Rav Kook raises for us is: Can I still be loving even while setting boundaries, even as I manifest a cooling or distancing of our relationship?

This is perhaps the most challenging aspiration in the writings of Rav Kook: How can we withhold love — with love? How can we stand in judgment — lovingly?

Rav Kook is guiding us to contextualize a moment that may be unpleasant. This moment of confrontation must not erase the entire relationship. I need to see this as only one specific moment in a long-term relationship. I shouldn't allow this present moment to erase the past and diminish the future of the relationship.

Rav Kook is guiding us to remain loving people even at the moment when our love is not overtly demonstrated.

Several years ago, such a conflict arose at a staff meeting at Ayeka, the organization I direct. One of our teachers, in front of all the

Can I still be loving even while setting boundaries, even as I manifest a cooling or distancing of our relationship?

SHK 3:31, 1:101

other staff members, spoke incredibly rudely to me. I was outraged. "Who the heck are you to talk to me like that?" I thought. "Don't you understand the structure of this organization? How could you have such chutzpah to speak so offensively to me? In front of everyone?!"

Looking back now, I realize that I didn't handle the interaction very well. I wasn't sure what to do. I didn't have a lot of experience being the director of an organization. I was hurt and infuriated. I told myself that this person was obviously immature, socially inept, and probably didn't get enough love as a child.

During all this, my chief concern was: How can I keep face as the head of an organization after being so embarrassed?

It was all about me. My love for this person had vanished the moment she began to speak. At that moment, I had no awareness of — or desire to sustain — a loving relationship.

Two years later, I faced a similar test, and this time, I fared a bit better. One of our employees found that our accountant had mishandled her pension. She became upset, and things got nasty. It is true that our accountant had made an oversight, but mistakes happen. We had known each other for years and had shared many satisfying moments. Her anger threatened to destroy our lengthy relationship.

This time I was able to let go of my outrage much more quickly. I sat down and wrote her a sincere letter of apology for the pain we had caused. I could have battled it out with her. Instead, we generously reimbursed her. My love for this person did not vanish in the fires of conflict.

When I look back on these two interactions, it is clear to me that when I managed to hold onto my love during the difficult conversations, the outcome was better for all concerned. Breathing love into the conflict sustained the relationship.

> It is clear to me that when I managed to hold onto my love during the difficult conversations, the outcome was better for all concerned. Breathing love into the conflict sustained the relationship.

Wandering Freely

What spark in these writings of Rav Kook resonates with you?

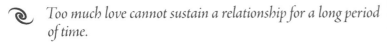 *Too much love cannot sustain a relationship for a long period of time.*

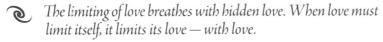 *The limiting of love breathes with hidden love. When love must limit itself, it limits its love — with love.*

Connecting to our Lives

☑ *What relationship of yours could benefit from clearer boundaries?*

☑ *Have you ever "limited love - lovingly"? What do you think was the key to accomplishing that?*

☑ *Who do you know who is skilled at setting healthy loving boundaries in relationships? Have a conversation with that person. Ask them how they do it. Ask them for advice.*

Loving Myself
Too Much

It may be hard to love ourselves, but on the other hand, can we love ourselves too much?

I've worked hard to forgive myself and forget my failings. I've worked hard to reframe my mess-ups and look at them as necessary opportunities for growth. I am finally a nine on a 1-to-10 scale of self-love.

But is there a shadow to this light? Should I always strive to love myself more, or is there a danger of too much self-love? Can loving myself become self-indulgent, narcissistic, or even destructive?

This natural quality of self-love is fraught with danger. It can intoxicate us. It can become addictive.

Firstly, it can limit our vision, such that we don't see beyond ourselves. We don't see the welfare of others or the community, the nation, or the world. We become so wrapped up in being chosen by God to play a unique role in this world that we wrap ourselves in a cocoon of self-absorption. When not balanced and contextualized, self-love can result in jealousy, comparison, hatred, and an endless number of negative qualities.

Yearning to Grow

When have I been too focused on myself?

The deepest fundamental flaw of love, including self-love, transpires when it is limited to only the self. Rav Kook saw this as a profound misunderstanding of both the world and a person's place in it.

He writes,

One's love for oneself can remain on its lowest level —
natural and primitive.
If it remains small,
it is liable to become destructive
and a springboard for harmful qualities and deeds.

Rav Kook was very concerned about "small love." Small love occurs when our love does not extend beyond our intimate circles — ourselves, our family, and our circle of friends. "Small love" does not include all the people who are outside this circle — the people with whom we have incidental contact, the people who are harder to get along with, and certainly not the larger picture of humanity. Small love occurs when we replace the question of "What is best for the world?" with "What is best for me?"

When love is not inclusive, the danger arises that we may regard people outside of our intimate circle as challenges — or even threats — to our loving circle. Small love can lead to impatience, manipulation, ruthless competition, and xenophobia. It can also be the source of anger, jealousy, grudge-holding, and possibly even revenge. Small love can create an "insider/outsider" mentality, suspicious of anyone not in the circle of insiders.

Cliques, fraternities, social groups, and even (especially) religions can breed an insider/outsider mentality. I remember how in the yeshiva I studied there was an unwritten law that we were different from the rest of the yeshiva world, and society as a whole; we were more modest and more virtuous. This was expressed in wearing socks with our sandals! It was our secret handshake, our code for identification

SHK 1:115

Small love occurs when we replace the question of "What is best for the world?" with "What is best for me?"

and separation. Our love for our group brought us to separate from and belittle other groups.

Secondly, too much self-love can result in an exaggerated sense of self. We may become preoccupied with our talents and oblivious to their effects on others.

Recently, an adult student remarked to me that she could not understand why she was not hired for a teaching position. After all, she had "dazzled" them in her pilot lesson. This expression is telling. "Dazzling" is an expression of too much light. It can be blinding. It neither enlightens nor elevates its beholders. In fact, it makes them feel smaller and inept. "Dazzling" may stem from the need to impress others with our self-worth, with our exceptionalism. It may be a symptom of "small love", of too much self-love.

Previously, we saw how Rav Kook thought of each individual as a single point in a pointillist painting. Each point is unique and essential. Each point graces the other points with its presence. But nevertheless, each point is substantial only insofar as it is seen in the context of the whole painting. Observed in the context of all the other points, the individual points create a beauty immeasurably more magnificent than any single point alone. But if one stands too close to a pointillist painting, focusing on individual points, no picture emerges; the points themselves seem incomplete. This "standing too close" is what Rav Kook calls "small love", witnessing only a few points, perhaps only *my* point, on the larger canvas.

Large love is seeing each individual point in the context of the whole picture of creation. Paradoxically, only this contextualization of our self-love can ultimately deepen and enrich our own love for ourselves. Only after we realize that we are each an essential "point" in the great painting of humankind can we fully appreciate our own place and significance. This is what Rav Kook would call "truly enlightened self-love."

Large love is seeing each individual point in the context of the whole picture of creation.

SHK 3:6

There is only the love of all being,
which is the truly enlightened and
supreme form of self-love.

According to Rav Kook, we cannot discover our full self-worth and meaning if we look exclusively at ourselves. When we do so, we end up loving a very limited version of ourselves, a very small form of loving. My love of myself can obscure my deeper self, which is connected to all beings.

Even worse, small love is a false sense of self-love. Rav Kook writes:

False self-love,
that which loves
only a tiny spark of my full self,
is a foolish form of self-deception.

If my love does not extend beyond myself, then even my love for myself is, in his words, false or "tiny". I am not loving my true self, which is destined to bring healing and *tikkun* to the larger world.

We cannot discover ourselves from within ourselves. Full self-love can be achieved only through an ever-expanding love for what is outside of us.

And when we reach the largest of those loves, the love of all being, then our love for ourselves becomes deeply authentic and enriching. Only when I grasp that I am part of a team effort involving all of humanity does my individual role become clear.

We cannot discover ourselves from within ourselves. Full self-love can be achieved only through an ever-expanding love for what is outside of us.

Wandering Freely

What spark in these writings of Rav Kook resonates with you?

🌀 *One's love for oneself can remain on its lowest level — natural and primitive. If it remains small, it is liable to become destructive and a springboard for harmful qualities and deeds.*

🌀 *There is only the love of all being, which is the truly enlightened and supreme form of self-love.*

🌀 *False self-love, that which loves only a tiny spark of my full self, is a foolish form of self-deception.*

Connecting to our Lives

☑ *Think of yourself as one point in a pointillist painting. What would the whole picture look like?*

☑ *How do you overcome the tendency to compare yourself to others?*

☑ *What is your most ludicrous ridiculous jealousy?*

☑ *Dedicate one full day to only say positive things about other people. Compliment them on even the smallest acts they do. How did you feel at the end of the day?*

Balancing Loving Others and Loving Myself

How can I become more supportive and loving of the successes of other people?

L et's return to our opening statement from Rav Kook's writings:

All of the Torah — ethics, mitzvot, learning, and practice —
come to remove the obstacles that prevent an
all-encompassing love from expanding and spreading
to every corner of life, everywhere.

What was Rav Kook referring to when he wrote "the obstacles that prevent an all-encompassing love from expanding and spreading to every corner of life, everywhere"?

What are these "obstacles"? Where do they come from? How did they enter into our lives? What holds us back? What prevents us from living a life of all-encompassing love?

If God has hardwired us to be loving creatures, then why don't we simply love all the time? A star does star-ness. A flower does flower-ness. An animal does animal-ness. They naturally express their inner beings. So, if the core of a human being is naturally flowing with love, then why aren't we always doing loving-ness? Everywhere? All the time? What gets in the way?

Why don't we love people more? One answer is that it's God's fault!

The primary obstacle to loving others isn't what happens to us in life. We may experience crises and disappointments that cause us to hold grudges, get angry, dislike and resent others, even gloat when others stumble. But all of these are symptoms of a much deeper, more problematic human predicament: We are hard-wired to be self-centered. We are hard-wired to prioritize looking out for ourselves.

In addition to the drive pushing us toward loving, connecting, and seeking harmony for all, God implanted within us a second drive, a very natural, persuasive, and potent drive to look out for ourselves — often at the expense of others. God gave each of us a unique personality and path so that we can bring much-needed healing to the world. God wants us to fulfill this purpose; God wants us to fulfill ourselves.

God has thus wired us with two opposing inner drives: one pushing us toward greater love, connection, and harmony; the other urging us to zealously seek to achieve our own potential.

Why did God give us this self-focused drive that so complicates our desire to become loving human beings?

Rav Kook writes,

> *The ultimate purpose of creation*
> *is the revealing of God's light in supreme oneness.*
> *Every single spark of life will fully actualize itself*
> *and ascend to full oneness*
> *and harmony with all other sparks.*
> *Then, all existence will shine in every detail of being,*
> *like prism light refracting in awe-inspiring beauty.*
> *To bring this about,*
> *all of creation had to be initially fractured into*
> *smaller and smaller discrete pieces,*
> *so that ultimately,*

God has wired us with two opposing inner drives: one pushing us toward greater love, connection, and harmony; the other urging us to zealously seek to achieve our own potential.

after the refinement and full realization
of each individual piece,
they could join together
in one beautiful and spiritual light.

SHK 1:902

Rav Kook is writing of a three-stage divine process in the progression of the world:

Stage 1: Originally, before the creation of the physical world, there was only God's perfect primordial light of undifferentiated oneness. It was all one unified light.

Stage 2: Then, as Rav Kook writes, "all of creation had to be fractured into smaller and smaller discrete pieces." The creation of this world entailed the breaking of God's perfect light of oneness into countless discrete individual pieces (sparks). These individual creations each need to go through a process of "refinement and full realization"; to fully become their whole selves, to actualize their potential. Imagine countless distinct and individual rays of light emerging from the oneness of the sun.

Stage 3: Finally, "after the refinement and full realization of each individual piece, they could join together in one beautiful and spiritual light." All the individual sparks unite in full spiritual harmony. Light rays refracting through a prism are more beautiful than a single undifferentiated beam of white light. So too, the beauty of the ultimately unified distinct lights will be infinitely more resplendent than that of the original, primordial, unified light.

Three stages. Of course, we are presently in stage 2, trying to "refine and fully realize" our own individual potential. Rav Kook adds,

Individuality needs to be fulfilled and expressed,
to enrich and beautify the exquisite composition of reality.
Each particular element of creation must fully emerge
and manifest its own unique essential and individual light.

Rav Kook is writing of a three-stage divine process in the progression of the world, culminating in greater harmony and beauty.

SHK 8:65

To accomplish this, God implanted within each of us a fierce and relentless drive to express and achieve our own individuality. It is neither selfish nor narcissistic to look out for ourselves. For the sake of the ultimate beauty and perfection of the world, we need to become ourselves.

It is thrilling to recognize that I am like no other, that I have a unique path. It fills me with hope and excitement. I exist; therefore, I am special. There is room for endless growth, endless potential, endless discovery. Imagine opening the door to greet your better self. Is there anyone in the world you would rather meet? Isn't this the greatest adventure in life?

It is my responsibility to "manifest my own unique essential and individual light". But this drive for individuation is difficult to control. It can lead us to passionately defend ourselves against anyone and anything that we perceive as a threat — anything that could possibly thwart the full realization of our potential. It can lead us to behavior antithetical to love, connection, and oneness; it can lead us to animosity, disconnection, and separation.

I once heard a beautiful example of this phenomenon from a fellow Jerusalemite, Rabbi David Aaron. He asked: "If unbeknownst to us we were cloned and we bumped into our cloned self — how would we feel about that clone?" He concluded that we would hate our cloned self more than anyone else in the world. A "second me" means that I, the original me, am now completely superfluous, utterly irrelevant. That would be the worst feeling in the world. I desperately want to have a unique path and purpose. I desperately *need* to be needed!

Rav Kook writes,

> *This (drive) explains the need for animosity…*
> *Animosity seeks to bring about full expression;*
> *ensuring that others —*

We are stuck between two contesting inner drives. We are hardwired for ongoing conflict, but at the same time, we are hardwired to love and connect.

---

personalities, peoples, assumptions and
characters, opinions and beliefs —
will not inhibit or usurp one's place.

SHK 8:65

The expressions of this drive — hatred, jealousy, holding a grudge, seeking revenge, judging others negatively — while utterly undesirable in and of themselves, represent the shadow side of the spiritual drive that God implanted in us. The first story outside of the Garden of Eden talks about Cain's tragic jealousy that led him to kill his brother Abel. This is the first and oldest story of what life is like outside of Paradise — life in the real world. We want and need to fulfill ourselves and so we perceive threats all around us.

We are stuck between these two contesting inner drives. We are hardwired for ongoing conflict. We endlessly compete and compare. At the same time, we are hardwired to love and connect. It's hard — really hard.

But though these two drives are often in conflict, they are both essentially good; they are both God-given. God implanted within us two drives that can so easily compete and undermine each other. One drive pushes us to love all of creation, to seek oneness with the animate and inanimate world. The other drive impels us to fulfill our own unique individuality, urging us to separate ourselves from all others and relentlessly strive to achieve our own potential.

We shouldn't fall into the trap of thinking that the drive for connection and harmony is good and the drive for self-fulfillment is bad. They are both necessary for the evolution and fulfillment of this world.

I felt this recently in synagogue on Shabbat morning. The guy sitting behind me was praying loudly and at a different pace than the rest of the community. It annoyed me to no end; I couldn't concentrate on my own praying with his voice buzzing in my ears. It was fine for him to pray at his own pace, but why did he have to do it so loudly?

One drive pushes us to love all of creation, to seek oneness with the animate and inanimate world. The other drive impels us to fulfill our own unique individuality, urging us to separate ourselves from all others and relentlessly strive to achieve our own potential.

I judged him harshly, telling myself that he was on an ego-trip, that he needed to convey to everyone that he was different; that his praying slower than the rest of the community reflected his being more spiritual and holy.

Then I remembered Rav Kook's thought of the two drives implanted within us and I realized that the man behind me perfectly illustrated both of these drives at the same moment. On the one hand, he felt a need to connect with other people and be part of the bigger picture, so he came to synagogue and prayed together with the community. And on the other hand, he needed to assert his own singular personality, to literally hear his own voice.

Though I was still irritated, Rav Kook's wisdom led me to understand and even celebrate his behavior (at least a little bit).

> If we allow the drive to love all of creation to dominate us, then we may never allow our own special unique light to shine. But when we focus exclusively on self-fulfillment, we shrink the whole universe down to our own single ray of light.

If we allow the drive to love all of creation to dominate us, then we may never allow our own special unique light to shine. We can lose our God-given individuality. We can silence our unique voice and fail to manifest our purpose in this world.

At the same time, when we focus exclusively on self-fulfillment, then the scope of our concern becomes small. We confine ourselves to a world limited to our own time, space, personal needs, and abilities. We shrink the whole universe down to our own single ray of light. In doing so, we diminish our capacity to connect to the infinite, the eternal, and the holy. We deny that part of us that yearns to connect to something much greater than ourselves.

In practical terms, when we allow the drive to fulfill our individual selves to govern our behavior, we will inevitably set up borders and barriers. Our love for ourselves will conflict with our love for others, causing us to prioritize ourselves and to differentiate ourselves from others. This differentiation zealously combats any force that is perceived as impeding, diminishing, or threatening the realization of our own potential. We will incessantly compare ourselves to others, and our life will become rife with jealousy. Tragically, when we fail to contextualize our loving, we can easily end up quite lonely. It is humbling, yet enthralling, to realize that we are each just one piece of the puzzle, one player on the team, one point in the painting.

The never-ending challenge in life is to listen to both of these compelling and competing drives, and to generate balance and harmony between them. To love both ourselves and all of creation — a quixotic seeking as elusive as it is sweet. The most fulfilling moments in life occur when we align our personal destiny with the prosperity and progress of the world. We feel connected to ourselves and at the same time connected to something much greater than ourselves. Inner and outer harmony. We own our authentic lives and also belong to something infinite, expansive, and holy.

The most fulfilling moments in life occur when we align our personal destiny with the prosperity and progress of the world.

Wandering Freely

What spark in these writings of Rav Kook resonates with you?

❧ *The ultimate purpose of creation is the revealing of God's light in supreme Oneness. Every single spark of life will fully actualize itself and ascend to full oneness and harmony with all other sparks. Then, all existence will shine in every detail of being, like prism light refracting in awe-inspiring beauty. To bring this about, all of creation had to be initially fractured into smaller and smaller discrete pieces, so that ultimately, after the refinement and full realization of each individual piece, they could join together in one beautiful and spiritual light.*

❧ *Individuality needs to be fulfilled and expressed, to enrich and beautify the exquisite composition of reality. Each particular element of creation must fully emerge and manifest its own unique essential and individual light.*

❧ *This (drive) explains the need for animosity. Animosity prevents other opinions and beliefs from diminishing the ultimate expression of each being. Animosity seeks to bring about full expression; ensuring that others — personalities, peoples, assumptions and characters, opinions and beliefs — will not inhibit or usurp its place.*

Connecting to our Lives

☑ *When you reflect on your moments of competition, jealousy, and perhaps even resentment toward others, how much of this do you think stemmed from your fear of being ordinary? Of having the other person diminish your light?*

☑ *Seek out two people you have been jealous of and compliment them (generously).*

Fear of Loving

L ife can beat us up.

Life can drain us — sometimes in dramatic ways; sometimes it can just slowly wear us down.

When we feel depleted, it can be very hard to remain aware of the love flowing through us. It is very hard to give love when we feel so desperately in need of *receiving* love. We yearn for someone to fill up our "love tank" when we are running on empty. It becomes difficult to direct our eyes outward toward others.

My cousin Helen taught me a huge lesson about loving. She had an infection in her legs that got worse and worse. The doctors were at their wits' end trying to find a way to heal her. Finally, adopting drastic measures, they performed an experimental operation. Afterward, she went into rehab for several months, confined to a wheelchair, and with the ominous possibility of having both legs amputated looming over her.

Helen had never married and had no family living near the rehabilitation center. She was alone, in a physically and emotionally daunting situation. Things seemed to be as dark as they could be.

Yearning to Grow

What worry, anxiety, or fear is it time to let go of?

But when I called her to ask how she was doing, she was upbeat. "I've been applying myself to help others," she said. "There is a man in our ward in a wheelchair who seems quite demoralized. So every day I wheel myself over to him, strike up a conversation, and try to lift his spirits. And you know what? After only a week, his mood has visibly lifted!"

Wow!

Sometimes, when we are in a dark place and feeling utterly depleted, we need to work hard to reframe our reality. When we do this, we may come to see that it's not random chance that we are in such a place. Maybe life has brought these troubles to our doorstep so that we can channel our love to someone who needs it even more. Even though we may think that our "love tank" is quite empty, there is always someone whose "love tank" is even emptier. When life beats us up, it is hard work not to collapse into a puddle of smallness and narrow self-interest. In the darkest of places, Helen's love brought her to connect and to give to others.

What can we learn from this? One lesson is that loving is expansive.

> For Rav Kook, the experience of love was continually about stretching boundaries and reaching out to others. He saw living a soulful life as being all about continually expanding the scope of connection and oneness, both toward God and toward all of creation.

For Rav Kook, the experience of love was continually about stretching boundaries and reaching out to others. One of the most frequently used words in his writings is "expansiveness" (*merchavim*). He saw living a soulful life as being all about continually expanding the scope of connection and oneness, both toward God and toward all of creation. The experience of loving brings us to a state of expansiveness, of open-armed inclusivity. Commentaries on the Talmud write that we manifest the extra soul we receive on Shabbat by inviting guests. Soulfulness is expansiveness.

Rav Kook's most famous poem is entitled "Expanses. Expanses," and depicts his yearning for unlimited growth and his consternation at any stifling restraint:

Expanses. Expanses.
Divine expansiveness my soul craves.
Confine me not in cages,
of substance nor of spirit.

SHK 3:279

Expanses. Expanses.

But how do we do it?

We expand by opening ourselves up to others. We look for the good in them. We reach out! Love reaches out even to strangers — people at the supermarket, waiting for the bus, parking lot attendants. Love pushes us to send good energy to all these people. We look them in the eye. We ask how they're doing. We care for them, with no thought of getting something in return. The Talmud says that we give tzedakah through showing our teeth to people, by smiling at them. And this loving in turn rebounds on us. We begin to glow, to smile at ourselves, to feel good.

During my many years of teaching in Jerusalem, I never had to ask my students when they were in love. Their faces shone with more light, their laugh was brighter, they exuded positive energy.

Loving is expansive. It is contagious. How many of us have felt at a wedding, when we see the new couple looking so lovingly at each other, a renewed sense of love for our own partners? How many of us have felt our love reignited when we look at our wedding albums?

And yet, for all his expansiveness, Rav Kook is apprehensive and cautious. He writes, "Confine me not in cages." What are these cages? What is Rav Kook worried about?

For Rav Kook, the primary cage — the primary force of confinement, limitation, restriction, and imprisonment — was fear. Fear stifles our growth. Fear extinguishes our loving.

We expand by opening ourselves up to others. We look for the good in them. We reach out!

While loving is expansive, fear is narrowing. While love urges us to connect with others, fear impels us to withdraw and go inside ourselves. Love is hopeful; fear is suspicious.

We are afraid of getting hurt, we are afraid of being vulnerable, we are afraid of giving more love than we receive. We are afraid that our emotions will be disregarded or crushed. We are afraid of being too animated and looking silly in front of others. We are afraid of letting go and loving expansively.

This fear, this stifling of our loving, starts at an early age. Sandra and I recently took our grandchildren to the zoo. While watching the monkeys, our four-year-old grandson could not restrain himself. He was bursting with uncontrolled joy. He simply loves the monkeys.

"What are you getting so excited about?" his elder sister said. "We've seen them before."

And just like that, his passion wilted. You could see him working very hard to curb his excitement and not express his unbridled love of the monkeys.

Fear teaches us to constrain our loving. Fear teaches us to be cautious.

Of course, there is a positive side to fear. Fear of God is one of the most praiseworthy qualities mentioned in the Torah. The proper dose and nuance of fear prevents us from rushing into places that may be physically or emotionally risky. Fear provides hesitation, prudence, and greater wariness. It can guard us against becoming too vulnerable and too emotionally raw. It can prevent us from getting hurt.

This same fear, this controlling of our desire to come closer to another, can also be a sign of respect for another human being. We do not need to know every inner secret. The positive side of our distancing prevents us from being overly curious or invasive. As the poet Rainer Maria Rilke writes, "Love consists in this: that two solitudes protect

> Love is hopeful; fear is suspicious. Fear teaches us to constrain our loving. Fear teaches us to be cautious.

and border and salute each other". (Letters to a Young Poet, 7)

What worried Rav Kook was not healthy fear and self-control. Every quality has its appropriate time and place. What worried Rav Kook was *excessive* fear.

> *Fear, when not properly refined,*
> *turns a person into a dish rag,*
> *a coward*
> *and a sham of himself.*

SHK 1:368

Fear can easily slide into excessive fear. Excessive fear does not just stifle us; it destroys us. It oppresses and tyrannizes us. It plays tricks with our heads and we begin to imagine every possible negative outcome. We exaggerate and invent worst-case scenarios. Everything looms as a slippery slope, leading to disaster. Excessive fear clogs our loving arteries like the worst kind of cholesterol. It is indeed a formidable cage.

Rav Kook writes,

> *Excessive fear*
> *takes away the spark of life of a person and all living beings.*
> *Nothing in the world is as bad and cruel as excessive fear.*
> *It increases all evils*
> *infinitely more than they actually are,*
> *it dims the beauty of all blessings in life,*
> *and pretends bad is present even when it is not.*
> *It paralyzes a person,*
> *who will refrain from doing anything positive.*
> *A person enters into a mindset of — "lest... " —*
> *until the person becomes weaker and weaker.*

What worried Rav Kook was not healthy fear and self-control. Every quality has its appropriate time and place. What worried Rav Kook was excessive fear.

Ikvei Hatzon

What happens to our loving when our fear grows into excessive fear? Answer: It stops.

Life teaches us to be careful, to be guarded. We learn how to restrain our loving. We learn how not to love.

How do we fine-tune this fear so that it does not become excessive? How do we not let fear "take away the spark of life"? What is the tikkun — the healing — of excessive fear?

Rav Kook writes,

> The eradicating of excessive fear
> will be accomplished through the opposite force,
> the power of chutzpah,
> that must become overpowering.
> Where there is chutzpah,
> there is no fear.

Rav Kook is not referring to the chutzpah of rude behavior, of cutting in line, or acting callously. He is calling for a higher level of antisocial behavior — of not being constrained by established norms and limitations. Not to let other people's expectations and conventions put us into a cage. An ideological chutzpah; a principled chutzpah. Chutzpah reflects the letting go of inhibitions and controls. It may be impulsive and outrageous. But on a deeper level, chutzpah is the breaking out of the cage that we build around ourselves. It is liberating.

Expansive loving is, at its essence, an audacious proposition. It takes a lot of courage to love. Even chutzpah.

Ikvei Hatzon

Expansive loving is, at its essence, an audacious proposition. It takes a lot of courage to love. Even chutzpah.

Wandering Freely

What spark in these writings of Rav Kook resonates with you?

- *Expanses. Expanses. Divine expansiveness my soul craves. Confine me not in cages, of substance nor of spirit.*

- *Fear, when not properly refined, turns a person into a dishrag, a coward and a sham of himself.*

- *Excessive fear takes away the spark of life of a person and all living beings. Nothing in the world is as bad and cruel as excessive fear. It increases all evils more infinitely than they actually are, dims the beauty of all blessings in life, and pretends bad is present even when it is not. It paralyzes a person, who will refrain from doing anything positive. A person enters into a mindset of — "lest" — until the person becomes weaker and weaker.*

- *The eradicating of excessive fear will be accomplished through the opposite force, the power of chutzpah, that must become overpowering. Where there is chutzpah — there is no fear.*

Connecting with our Lives

☑   *Take a day to notice and compliment at least five people with whom you usually do not interact. Notice their reactions. How does this make you feel about yourself?*

☑   *What frightens you about loving openly and generously? What is holding you back from loving more audaciously?*

☑   *Notice any personal cynicism or diminishing of the exuberance of others. How do you feel when you put the brakes on another person's enthusiasm?*

☑   *What act of outrageous, fearless chutzpah (in a positive sense) could you do today?*

Being Stuck

And so we come to one final obstacle to loving. I want to be a loving person, but sometimes it's just so hard to actually be the person I want to be. I don't want to be a small person, a self-absorbed person. But sometimes it's hard for me to get beyond the predicament, the state of being, that I am trapped in.

I'm not wallowing in self-pity, but still, I am stuck.

How can I de-stuckify myself?

How can I better listen to the wisdom of my soul, the voice that is perpetually urging me to become a force of oneness in the world? How can I get back on track? How can I do a personal recalibration, attuning myself to become more expansive? To be more loving? To channel the love that flows naturally from my soul?

What should I do when I become overwhelmed by the obstacles to loving? What should I do when fear, worry, anxiety, hurt, lack of self-worth, or just life diminish my capacity to love?

Rav Kook would say that "soul alignment" occurs during prayer — serious prayer.

Rav Kook was a prayerful personality. His primary disciple, Rav David HaCohen, popularly known as the Nazir, chose to become Rav Kook's student after he heard him pray in the adjoining room of their hotel in Switzerland. The Nazir heard the melody of serious prayer and was enraptured.

Rav Kook writes,

> *The soul is always praying.*
> *When many days or years have passed*
> *without serious prayer,*
> *toxic stones gather around one's heart,*
> *and one feels because of them*
> *a certain heaviness of spirit.*

Olat HaRa'aya, Introduction

We need to continually realign ourselves and tap into the animating force of our soul. We have to stop and listen to ourselves, to the voice of our souls.

"Toxic stones gather around one's heart ... heaviness of spirit". These "stones" dull our energy and narrow the scope of our concern for others. They shrink our lives; they deplete us and make our lives a heavy burden to carry.

The painful reality Rav Kook is conveying to us is: unless we engage in "serious prayer", toxic stones will inevitably gather around our hearts. They will accumulate, higher and wider, until we must struggle to access our innermost being. They will drain our vital energy. We need to continually realign ourselves and tap into the animating force of our soul, which lies deep and often concealed within us. In short, we have to stop and listen to ourselves, to the voice of our souls. To listen deeply, without an agenda.

When Rav Kook writes of "serious prayer", he is not talking about organized, formal, public prayer. He is not referring to the times of day when a traditional Jew would pray, nor to the words of the prayer book. He is referring to personal soulful prayer which, in his eyes, was primarily a focused hearkening to the inner voice of the soul. A prayer of attentive listening. A prayer of openness and vulnerability, inviting divine wisdom to come to us through our inner voice. This serious prayer is a pause in directing our energy outward; it is an inner realignment that involves directing our energy inward, to become more present with ourselves.

Not to be confused with meditation, "serious prayer" for Rav Kook is not about achieving a sense of serenity or tranquility. "Serious prayer" is a preparation to receive soulful guidance and be a catalyst for personal growth and action. "Serious prayer" can happen at any time, in any place, for any person.

Rav Kook writes that our soul is always communicating to us; it is always whispering and singing and praying to us. It conveys its message to us, sometimes through flashes of insight, what he refers to as "soulful lightning bolts", and sometimes through subtle intuitions. It suggests what steps we should take in our lives. It enlightens our path. "Serious prayer" is the hearing of the prayer of our soul, which is constantly trying to break through to us.

He writes:

> *Waves from the higher realm*
> *act on our souls ceaselessly.*
> *The stirrings of our inner spiritual sensibilities*
> *are the result of the sounds released*
> *by the violin of our souls,*
> *as it listens to the echo*
> *of the sounds emanating*
> *from the divine realm.*

"Serious prayer" is hearing of the prayer of our soul, which is constantly trying to break through to us.

SHK 8:15

Serious prayer is the "listening to the waves from the higher realm acting on our souls," of "listening to the soul which is always praying," of channeling how God wants us to live in this world. When, for whatever reasons, we do not, or cannot, experience serious prayer, then "toxic stones gather around [our] heart." Toxic stones are the obstacles that impede and limit our loving. They create "a certain heaviness of spirit," a spiritual sluggishness, an inability to be fully alive and expansive.

Serious prayer is the medium that enables me to better listen to the voice of my soul. Serious prayer helps to remove the obstacles clogging the pathways of my soul. Serious prayer refocuses me on how to grow into the person I want to be. Serious prayer helps me reveal what is truly happening inside of me.

In short, serious prayer is the gateway to becoming more loving.

Once we understand that the soul is constantly inviting us to become forces of Oneness — to become more loving human beings — then there is really only one prayer: "Please God, help me to remove the obstacles that inhibit my loving. Please God, give me the strength and wisdom to become a more loving human being". Everything else — all other thoughts, speech, and actions — stem from this one single aspiration.

Our deepest prayer reveals to us our deepest desire, in full vulnerability and yearning. Paradoxically, when we experience "serious prayer", when we listen to the inner voice of our soul and pray with full yearning and vulnerability, our prayers are answered. We somehow mysteriously unlock something within ourselves and discover the strength and wisdom we need. The willingness to express our deepest longings and hopes wakes us up to the next step on the road to our becoming more loving people.

The result of this process should be the reawakening of our inner lives and a deepening of our capacity and power to become more loving human beings.

We restore love for this world through prayer.

The willingness to express our deepest longings and hopes wakes us up to the next step on the road to our becoming more loving people.

SHK 1:467

Wandering Freely

What spark in these writings of Rav Kook resonates with you?

🌀 *The soul is always praying. When many days or years have passed without serious prayer, toxic stones gather around one's heart, and one feels because of them a certain heaviness of spirit... Prayer is only truly genuine when it arises from the awareness that the soul is always praying.*

🌀 *Waves from the higher realm act on our souls ceaselessly. The stirrings of our inner spiritual sensibilities are the result of the sounds released by the violin of our souls, as it listens to the echo of the sound emanating from the divine realm.*

🌀 *We restore love for this world through prayer.*

Connecting to our Lives

☑ *What do you think is the prayer that your soul is praying to you now?*

☑ *Go outside, find a quiet place, and start talking to God. Talk for at least 15 minutes. Begin with "Dear God, it's been a while since we've talked, but this is what is on my mind …." Try to be as vulnerable as you can. What did you hear?*

☑ *What do you do to "de-stuckify" yourself?*

Conclusion

"The Torah is love"

Loving is never easy.

It is not easy to love others. It is not easy to love ourselves. But how many of us have ever said to ourselves: "I need to grow in my loving. I need to expand my loving"? How many of us have ever asked ourselves: "How can I become a more loving human being?"

Of all the realms of self-improvement, this may be the most essential one today. Perhaps this is what we need, more than anything else. We need to bring more loving into this beautiful and broken world.

We are living in a time of conditional love.

We are living in a time of uncontrolled anger and judgmentalism.

We are living in a time of unparalleled loneliness.

When I married Sandra, I told her that I loved her. No one ever whispered to me that I could always love her even more. There is no limit to love.

Where do I go to become a more loving human being?

I know where to go if I want to get into better physical shape. I find a good physical trainer.

I know where to go if I want to heal myself emotionally. I find a good therapist.

I know where to go if I want my career to take off. I find a good life coach.

I know where to go if I want to feel better physically. I find a good doctor.

I know where to go if I want to fix my car, or my teeth, or my hearing.

But where do I go if I want to grow in my loving? Where do I find a good "loving coach"?

For me, it was Rav Kook.

Rav Kook gave me the awareness, wisdom, and courage to notice how narrow and inadequate my loving was. He inspired me to ask my wife and children the most vulnerable questions I have ever asked: "Do you feel loved enough? What do you need from me to make you feel more loved?"

One of Rav Kook's most simple and perhaps most astonishing sentences is:

The Torah is love.

The Torah is love.

The Torah is not only the story of the Jewish People. It is not only our legal, moral, and spiritual guide. It is more than all of that. The Torah is the expression of God's love for us. Which we then channel to others and to the whole world. It should make us feel loved; we are God's beloved.

A long time ago I met someone who had learned with Rav Kook.

The Torah is not only the story of the Jewish People. It is not only our legal, moral, and spiritual guide. It is more than all of that. The Torah is the expression of God's love for us. Which we then channel to others and to the whole world.

SHK 1:226

I was feeling a bit snarky, and so I asked him: "There are so many rabbis, what made Rav Kook so special?" He floored me with his answer: "When you met Rav Kook, all of a sudden you realized that Judaism worked".

Wow!

It wasn't his erudition or eloquence or even his behavior. There was an aura. Meeting him was inspirational. Meeting him was transformative. I would say that this aura stemmed from his accessing the loving that flowed from his soul. It washed away walls, inhibitions, and fears.

I think that the question I asked Sandra and our kids is really the question we need to wake up with each day and ask the world: "Do you feel loved enough? What do you need from me now to feel more loved?"

And if the world were to ask me: "What do you love about me?" I hope my answer would be: "Everything. Every cell. Every moment. All of you."

If the world were to ask me: "What do you love about me?" I hope my answer would be: "Everything. Every cell. Every moment. All of you."

Connecting to our Lives

☑ *Sit comfortably and close your eyes. Imagine that you are loved by God. Imagine that the whole universe loves you. Your existence is needed in this world. How do you feel?*

☑ *Who do you need to ask: "What do you need from me to feel more loved?"*

☑ *What would you answer if the world were to ask you: "What do you love about me?"*

Acknowledgments

This book is the fruit of my blessed engagement with the Ayeka online community. We started meeting weekly several years ago. Who could have dreamed that we would create a sacred space of trust, support, integrity, and compassion? What began as a four-session series at the beginning of COVID, focusing on Rav Kook's approach to love, eventually metamorphosed into years of exploration of the depth, originality, creativity, and beauty of his thought. Thank you fellow Ayeka-ites, you have enriched my life infinitely.

The Ayeka team of Yehoshua Looks, Michal Fund, Mick Weinstein, Stuart and Sara Meyers, have been kindred spirits, offering wisdom and support every step of the way.

Emily Wichland, Rabbi Tzvi Sinensky, Esther Frumkin, and Sarina Furer — if this book is readable and has a trace of grace, the credit is yours.

Kasva Press — Yael and Don — what can I say? You guided the journey of this book, both big picture and small details, with wisdom and insight. Every moment working together has been a pleasure.

This whole project of developing an online soulful community would not have been possible without the generous support of the Jim Joseph Foundation. A special shout-out to Stacie and Dawne.

David K. — what can I say? For years now we have studied Rav Kook's *Shemoneh Kvatzim* together. What a journey. Sometimes understanding everything; sometimes not understanding anything. But always opening our souls together, seeking to explore and grow and allow ourselves to receive his light. Every moment has been a taste of the world to come.

Finally, it should be noted that the translations in this book are all mine. Rav Kook's Hebrew is poetic and lyrical, impossible to capture in translation. If anything, I hope this book inspires its readers to turn to the original sources of Rav Kook's writings.